"Let marriage experts Drs. Les and Leslie Parrott help you "trade up" to a great marriage. *Trading Places* will not only inspire you but will also give you the tools you need to see life through your partner's eyes. If you're looking for more understanding, intimacy, and empathy in your marriage, this book is written especially for you. A must-read!"

Claudia & David Arp, authors
of the 10 Great Dates series.

"*Trading Places* offers a ticket to vastly improved marital intimacy and is well worth the price of admission. The Parrotts' trademark use of fascinating and groundbreaking research provides unusual depth and substance. To top it all off, it's a delightful read as well."

Gary Thomas, author of *Sacred Marriage*
and *Sacred Influence*

Les and Leslie Parrott are nothing short of inspirational. Practical and challenging, *Trading Places* reminded me of "the secret" of marital happiness and success. A regular dose of the Parrotts' writing has done wonders for me personally and for my marriage.

Jim Burns, PhD, president of HomeWord
and author of *Creating an Intimate Marriage*
and *Confident Parenting*

"*Trading Places* by the Parrotts gives couples a road map on how to connect heart-to-heart through experiencing and practicing the art of empathy in their marriage. A must-read."

Dr. Gary and **Barb Rosberg**,
America's Family Coaches, authors of
The 5 Sex Needs of Men & Women,
cohosts of *Dr. Gary and Barb: Your Marriage
Coaches*, and nationally known speakers

Resources by Les and Leslie Parrott

Books

Becoming Soul Mates
The Complete Guide to Marriage Mentoring
Getting Ready for the Wedding
I Love You More (and workbooks)
Just the Two of Us
L.O.V.E. (and workbooks)
Love Is . . .
The Love List
Love Talk (and workbooks)
Meditations on Proverbs for Couples
The Parent You Want to Be
Pillow Talk
Questions Couples Ask
Relationships (and workbook)
Saving Your Marriage Before It Starts (and workbooks)
Saving Your Second Marriage Before It Starts (and workbooks)
Trading Places (and workbooks)
51 Creative Ideas for Marriage Mentors

Video Curriculum — ZondervanGroupware®

Complete Resource Kit for Marriage Mentoring
I Love You More
Love Talk
Saving Your Marriage Before It Starts

Audio

Love Talk
Saving Your Marriage Before It Starts
Saving Your Second Marriage Before It Starts

Books by Les Parrott

The Control Freak
Crazy Good Sex
Helping Your Struggling Teenager
High Maintenance Relationships
The Life You Want Your Kids to Live
Seven Secrets of a Healthy Dating Relationship
Shoulda, Coulda, Woulda
Once Upon a Family
3 Seconds
25 Ways to Win with People (coauthored with John Maxwell)
Love the Life You Live (coauthored with Neil Clark Warren)

Books by Leslie Parrott

The First Drop of Rain
If You Ever Needed Friends, It's Now
You Matter More Than You Think
God Loves You Nose to Toes (children's book)
Marshmallow Clouds (children's book)

THE SECRET TO THE MARRIAGE
YOU WANT

TRADING
PLACES

DRS. LES & LESLIE PARROTT

 ZONDERVAN®   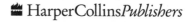 HarperCollins*Publishers*

ZONDERVAN.com/
AUTHORTRACKER
follow your favorite authors

ZONDERVAN

Trading Places
Copyright © 2008 by The Foundation for Healthy Relationships

This title is also available as a Zondervan audio product.
Visit www.zondervan.com/audiopages for more information.

Requests for information should be addressed to:

Zondervan, *Grand Rapids, Michigan 49530*

This edition: ISBN 978-0-310-32779-0 (softcover)

Library of Congress Cataloging-in-Publication Data

Parrott, Les.
    Trading places : the best move you'll ever make in your marriage / Les & Leslie
Parrott.
        p.   cm.
    Includes bibliographical references.
    ISBN 978-0-310-27246-5 (hardcover)
    1. Marriage — Religious aspects — Christianity. I. Parrott, Leslie L., 1964- II. Title.
BV835.P37   2008
    248.8'44 — dc22   2007044686

Published in association with Yates & Yates, www.yates2.com.

Interior design by Beth Shagene

Printed in the United States of America

10 11 12 13 14 15 • 23 22 21 20 19 18 17 16 15 14 13 12 11 10 9 8 7 6 5 4 3 2

To Kevin and Kathy Lunn

A couple adept at trading places,
and a couple we love dearly.

* Do you know the single most important secret to a happy marriage?
* Do you want to reduce critical comments and eliminate nagging forever?
* Do you want to know how to get what you really want—starting today?
* Would you like to short-circuit conflict before it even begins?
* Would you like to ignite more passion in your bedroom?
* Are you ready to go beneath the surface for a deeper connection?

If so, you're ready for *Trading Places*.

Contents

Acknowledgments

As always, we are so grateful to the following people who make up our publishing team: Scott Bolinder, Bruce Ryskamp, Stan Gundry, Joyce Ondersma, Jackie Aldridge, Mark Hunt, John Raymond, T. J. Rathbun, Jeff Bowden, Michael Ranville, Sandy Vander Zicht, Becky Shingledecker, Sealy Yates, Kevin Small, Bill Dallas, Terry Rouch, and Janice Lundquist. We will never be able to say thank you enough.

> Mutual empathy
> is the great unsung
> human gift.
>
> **Jean Baker Miller**

Walking in Your Partner's Shoes

More than any other single deficiency,
I think it is the lack of mutual empathy
which results in sword-drawing in marriage.
Bernard Guerney

"Our viewers want to know the most important thing they can do for their marriage," the producer told us. We were sitting in plush leather chairs, sipping bottled water out of straws in the green room of the famous Harpo Studios in Chicago. "Oprah is likely to ask you," the producer continued, "if you could only give one suggestion to a couple for improving their marriage, what would it be?"

We didn't have to think twice.

In fact, it wasn't the first time we'd been asked. We hear this question a lot. In nearly every interview we do on marriage, whether it's print, radio, or television, that question is predictable.

Why? Probably because, regardless of the topic, we all like to get to the heart of the matter. Think about it. Wouldn't you like to know the most important thing you can do ... to keep your kids off drugs ... to save more time ... to extend your life ... to make a perfect soufflé ... to stop global warming ... to get a promotion?

Whatever the topic, we like to know the *one* key thing. What matters most? What's the essential element, that indispensable and vital factor for success?

Well, when it comes to that crucial component in a successful marriage, there's no need to guess. We stand on a mountain of research and clinical expertise when we tell you the answer. In a word, it's *empathy*. It's putting yourself in your partner's shoes. The happiest couples on earth are those who become adept at trading places.

Ignorance Is Bliss?

When a couple neglects to trade places, when they sidestep empathy, they become clueless. Quite literally, they become ignorant of each other. Their lack of awareness causes them to flounder. They say things like:

- "I have no idea what would make him happy."
- "I simply do not understand her."
- "He gets angry for absolutely no reason."
- "We'll just be talking and then she blows up at me."
- "He stopped listening to me and I have no idea why."
- "I cannot understand why she keeps talking about this."

These are the sayings of a clueless couple. Like a gas gauge edging toward "empty," these statements indicate an embarrassingly low level of empathy. Yet the empathy deficit goes unnoticed. They don't recognize what they're missing. On the other hand, these kinds of statements also show a lack of *apathy*. And that's a good thing. Couples who say these sorts of things still care. They still crave a better way of living and loving together. They're simply baffled by their spouse's feelings, thoughts, and behaviors. They're oblivious. Clueless.

> **clue** ('klü): anything that serves to guide or direct in the solution of a problem.

Truth be told, we're all clueless as couples some of the time. Every husband and wife, no matter how loving, has moments of mystery—moments when we can't begin to understand each other. "What are you thinking?" we may ask in astonishment. Or, "I can't believe you'd say that!" Each and every couple, from time to time, becomes perplexed and bemused by each other.

And that's precisely why every couple, regardless of their age or stage, will never make a more important move in their marriage than when they trade places. Why? Because ignorance about your partner's thoughts, feelings, and motives is definitely not bliss. It's the furthest thing from it. If anything, empathy is bliss!

Now, if all this sounds like hyperbole to you, we apologize. It's just that we know what a bit more empathy can do for your marriage. In fact, it's difficult to exaggerate the importance and value of empathy to a strong and happy marriage. Why? Because whenever we put ourselves in our partner's shoes, we become educated. We push back ignorance. We understand each other. And, at the risk of sounding trite, our understanding helps us love. That's why we

> The greatest obstacle to discovery is not ignorance—it's the illusion of knowledge.
>
> Daniel J. Boorstin

don't have to think twice about our answer to the question: What's the most important thing a couple can do for their marriage?

Trade places, if only for a minute.

It's that simple—and that difficult.

Trading Places Is Easier Than You Think

Let's not kid anyone. Empathy is not always easy. That's why we've written this book. But as you are about to discover, empathy can be easier than you think. In fact, it can become downright habit-forming. We intend to show you, step by step, how you can practice this essential skill to reduce conflict, improve communication, heighten your intimacy, and even fire up your love life. Once you experience the rewards of trading places, we're convinced you'll be a true believer in its importance.

Here's a quick overview of what's to come:

- In part 1 of the book, we explore the basics, the very rudiments, of trading places. You can consider this first section part pep talk, part action plan, and part prerequisite to the benefits you'll soon enjoy. We'll show you exactly what it means to trade places, and how it can become a routine habit in your own marriage. We'll also take a close look at the "admission ticket" trading places requires of every couple.

- In part 2, we roll up our proverbial sleeves and give you exactly what you'll need to trade places. In fact, we are going to give you "three easy steps" to practicing empathy. We cringe as we write this phrase, "three easy steps," because it sounds so trite. But trust us, we have our reasons. For now, think of it as "simplicity on the other side of complexity." Empathy, after all, is one of the most profound and challenging behaviors you'll ever accomplish. That's why in this portion of the book, we go out of our way to make it as simple and memorable as possible.

- Part 3 is going to help you drill down deep in a few specific areas of your marriage — areas where you are most likely to find the richest rewards. In fact, you can think of this section of the book as an insider's guide. If you were just starting out in the oil business, think how valuable it would be to have someone map out for you exactly where you should place your drills for the greatest supply of oil. This section is a bit like that map. We want you to strike it rich with understanding, and that's why we're going to show you precisely where to drill down with your newly honed empathy skills.

Getting the Most from This Book

If you've read some of our other books, like *Love Talk, Saving Your Marriage Before It Starts, I Love You More,* or *Your Time-Starved Marriage,* you know that we like to provide our readers with as many tools as possible for putting our message into practice. That's why, once again, we're providing you with additional ways to augment your learning experience with this book. Both them are merely options.

First, you'll notice that each chapter includes questions for reflection. These take only a few minutes to ponder and are expressly designed to help you think through and apply what you've read.

Second, at the end of each chapter, we'll reference a workbook exercise. You have the option of using the men's and women's workbooks as you go through *Trading Places.* These workbooks aren't required; they are simply available as an aid for making the material more personal to you and your relationship if you think it would be helpful. They contain self-tests to fill out and exercises to do together.

> Two parts of empathy: skill (tip of iceberg) and attitude (mass of the iceberg).
> **Anonymous**

For now, we want you to know that when you make trading places a common occurrence in your marriage, you're guaranteed to be more understanding—and more understood. In other words, you'll be more loving and you'll feel more loved.

PART ONE

THE ESSENTIALS OF TRADING PLACES

On a flight from Seattle to Houston, where Les and I were scheduled to speak at a marriage conference, the airline lost our luggage. After describing the size and shape of our bags, the attendant took our claim check and proceeded to a back room.

"I'm sorry," he said upon his return, "your bags will probably come in on the next flight and be delivered to your hotel sometime tomorrow afternoon."

"We'll already be on our way back to Seattle by that time," Les said.

"That's okay," the attendant responded. "We can have the bags rerouted back to Sea-Tac for you."

"How kind," Les murmured under his breath.

"Well, anyway, here's an essentials kit to help you out," the man said as he slid a little zippered bag across the countertop in our direction.

On the side of the bag, no bigger than a baked potato, was the logo of the airline, and in all caps was the word *ESSENTIALS*. The little bag contained miniature items like a toothbrush and toothpaste, deodorant, shampoo, and tissues.

"So *these* are the 'essentials,'" Les said as we were walking away from the counter. "I guess we overpacked."

Well, in a sense, part 1 of this book is a bit like that "essentials" bag. Here we are going to give you prerequisites for trading places.

It's not all you need to know or do, but it's enough information to get you started.

- In chapter 1, "The Two Sides of Trading Places," you'll discover in plain language what mutual empathy is. In fact, you'll see a graphic depiction of the essential ingredients that go into every effective act of trading places, and we'll help you determine your personal "empathy quotient."

- Next, in "What Trading Places Will Do for Your Marriage," we'll show you the rich rewards your empathic efforts will pay you. You just may be surprised by how sweet your life can be when you practice this time-tested technique. Truly, the rewards of trading places are many.

- The final chapter in this section, "The Prerequisite for Trading Places," uncovers what most people never figure out about cultivating genuine empathy for their spouse. In all honesty, we've seen countless couples attempt to put themselves in each other's shoes but fail miserably because they never got a lock on the key element we reveal in this chapter.

So let's get started and take a good look at the "essentials" of trading places.

CHAPTER 1

The Two Sides
of Trading Places

*If there is any great secret of success in life,
it lies in the ability to put yourself in the other person's place
and to see things from his point of view —
as well as your own.*

Henry Ford

"Before you leave this auditorium, we want you to pick up a small bottle you'll find on a table in the foyer. Open it once you get home and pour it on your relationship. It's a bottle of empathy."

We've often dreamed of being able to say something like this to the groups of couples who come to our marriage seminars. Wouldn't it be terrific if trading places could be just that easy; if you could open a bottle and apply some kind of ointment to your marriage, and then instantly enjoy the relief and pleasure that come from mutual empathy?

How much would you pay for a bottle? It's a moot question, of course. Empathy is not a tangible commodity you can pick up at a local drugstore. But it is an invaluable asset. If it were sold in a retail outlet, we think it would probably be offered at only the finest of stores, and probably kept in a vault. Why? Because empathy is precious and rare. Its value is impossible to calculate.

Think of the rewards you'd reap in your relationship if you could, at any given moment, instantly apply a dose of mutual empathy to your interaction. Imagine how it would improve your ability to make decisions together, to work as a team, overcome hardship, achieve goals, and enjoy physical intimacy. In short, imagine how a ready measure of mutual empathy would elevate your happiness and forever join your spirits.

If you could both see the world from each other's point of view, instantly and routinely, what would your marriage look like? In other words, what would you use your bottle of instant empathy to accomplish in your marriage?

> **em·pa·thy** ('em-pə-thē): The identification with and understanding of another's situation, feelings, and motives.

We can tell you how we'd answer that question.

Our marriage would have more laughter and less bickering. We'd use our bottle of empathy to become more adept at reading one another. We'd offer each other more care and comfort. We'd use it to create a warm emotional space while playing together with our kids. With an abundance of mutual empathy, we'd have fewer hurt feelings and a lot more fun. We'd have conversations that required little effort and afforded us moments of deep understanding. We'd be more thoughtful. More protective. More considerate. More indulgent of each other's quirks. Less judgmental and a lot more perceptive. We'd use instant empathy when we needed to lay down our pride and become more patient with each other. And when trying to muster the courage to apologize or ask forgiveness, we'd offer each other an abundance of grace. We'd never spend a minute letting the other feel left out or scared. We'd give more compliments. We'd show more gratitude. With more empathy, we'd dare to dream bigger dreams together. We'd share our secret hopes. We'd hold each other longer and more frequently. We'd kiss more passionately. We'd smile at each other more often. In short, if we could instantly and routinely apply a dose of mutual empathy to our marriage whenever we chose, we'd have more love.

Make no mistake—empathy is at the heart of love. No other practice can do more for your marriage than empathy. Yet too many couples neglect it at their peril. Why? Because they've never learned the secret to putting it into practice. And that's exactly what we intend to reveal to you through this chapter.

The secret is found in your head and in your heart. Literally.

Brain-to-Brain and Heart-to-Heart

We recently sat around an ordinary conference table in Southern California with six of the most prestigious relationship researchers in the country. The group was called together by Dr. Galen Buckwalter. Our purpose? To share our thoughts on what some are calling the new science of "neural calculus."

Now, before we lose you at the very utterance of this mind-numbing phrase, hang in there for just a moment.

We're not about to give you a heady lesson on social neuroscience. We simply want you to know that what you are about to learn in this book is new. Sure, empathy is as old as time, but not the way we're going to look at it. Why? Because something new and exciting is beginning to brew in some of the most respected university research laboratories in North America. It's not a cure for a biological disease, but it just may be a cure for whatever's ailing your marriage. And it promises to be revolutionary. We don't say that glibly. We genuinely believe that you are about to learn the rudiments of a practice that will positively impact your marriage in countless ways. It's a proven fact.

You see, until now, neuroscience has studied just one brain at a time. But now two are being analyzed at once, unveiling a never-before-seen neural duet between the brains of a husband and wife as they interact.[1] That's what's meant by the phrase "neural calculus." So why does this matter? Because this emerging new science holds startling implications for your marriage. It holds revolutionary secrets for bonding the two of you brain-to-brain and heart-to-heart — quite literally.

> I try to hear things through the ears of others, and see things through their eyes.
>
> **Leonard Riggio**

In fact, Carl Marci of Harvard University has extracted from his extensive data something he calls a "logarithm for empathy."[2] It's all about the interplay of two people as they enjoy a deep connection of rapport. Not only that, his logarithm reduces the pattern of two people's physiology at the peak of rapport — where each feels deeply understood by the other — to a mathematical equation. Imagine that!

Don't worry, we're not about to extrapolate a numerical equation for empathy here. But we want to lift the curtain on a practice that offers you a near guarantee for a pleasurable, engaging, and smooth marriage. It's a practice that generates harmony and strengthens the bonds between you, no matter what the state of your marriage may be.

What It Means to Trade Places

Let's define what we're talking about. *Empathy* means imagining what life is like at a moment in time for your spouse. It means putting yourself in your spouse's skin, looking at life through their eyes. It means walking in their shoes. When you do this for your spouse and your spouse does this for you, you're *trading places*.

The point of empathy is to understand your spouse's feelings, desires, ideas, and actions at a meaningful level. In a sense, its goal is to momentarily *become* your partner. It's what poet Walt Whitman was getting at back in 1855 when he wrote his masterwork *Leaves of Grass*: "I do not ask the wounded person how he feels; I, myself *become* the wounded person" (italics mine).

Now trading places requires *mutual* empathy. It's not one-sided.* It's reciprocal. And it doesn't keep score. It hones in on *moments of marital brilliance* where your connection is intense, vivid, and radiant. Almost sacred—a marital communion. But it's not relegated to rarity. Trading places can be a common occurrence and a frequent experience in your marriage. No need to leave these moments to chance or fate. Once you learn the secrets to trading places, you'll see just how quickly this practice can be cultivated.

> The great gift of human beings is that we have the power of empathy.
>
> **Meryl Streep**

But keep in mind that these moments begin with one of you practicing empathy.

We also like to think about empathy with the word *attunement*. It's a word that actually has musical connotations—meaning to be in tune or in harmony. And that's exactly what empathy does in our relationship. It enables us to be in tune with each other and to live in harmony. We now want to reveal something vitally important about empathy that most couples don't realize.

---

*If your marriage is going through a particularly tough spot right now where your partner isn't motivated to see life from your point of view, we encourage you to read appendix A before moving to the next chapter. We have some special suggestions for you as you read the remainder of this book.

The Secret Most Couples Don't Know

The dictionary defines empathy as "the identification with and understanding of another's situation, feelings, and motives." But what it doesn't tell you is how easily empathy can be mistaken for much less than this. And it doesn't tell you that empathy requires two sides.

Here's the secret most miss: Empathy calls for loving your partner with both your head and heart, concurrently. Most of us do one or the other pretty well; we either feel our partner's pain with our heart, or we try to solve their problem with our head. To do both can be tricky. But that's the request of empathy.

When you trade places with your spouse, when you truly empathize with him or her, you are using both your analytical skills, that is, your cognitive understanding, as well as your sympathetic skills, or your emotional resonance. In short, you're using both your head and your heart.

> The heart has its reasons, that reason does not know.
>
> Blaise Pascal

Most couples never understand the implications of this insight. You see, some of us are programmed to "trade places" intellectually, using our head to analyze the circumstances of our partner. I (Les) do this whenever I nobly spell out Leslie's issues by saying things like, "If you didn't get so emotional about this problem, you might just see that it's not that bad." Is this objective observation true? It may be. But it's not empathy. And in most cases it's not even helpful.

Others of us are more inclined to "trade places" emotionally, using our heart to sympathize with our partner's position. I (Leslie) do this with compassion and sensitivity when I sidle up to Les and say things like, "I know you're feeling discouraged and I really hurt for you." Is this subjective surveillance accurate? Perhaps. Les may, indeed, be feeling discouraged. But maybe not. And in either case, it's not empathy.

Both approaches are pale imitations of empathy. But know this: when these two approaches come together, true empathy takes flight. Like two wings of an airplane, empathy requires both your head and your heart to get off the ground.

> It is only as we fully understand opinions and attitudes different from our own and reasons for them that we better understand our own place in the scheme of things.
>
> **S. I. Hayakawa**

When we attempt to trade places primarily with our head, we are merely analyzing. And when we trade places only with our heart, we are merely sympathizing. Of course, there's nothing wrong with either. But don't mistake them for empathy.

The Trading Places Matrix

If you could X-ray empathy, what would it look like? We've actually given this question, strange as it may sound, a great deal of thought. We've literally discussed it for years, most of our married life. It all began when we were both in graduate school. Les was conducting a massive psychological study for his doctoral dissertation on empathy. And as any PhD student can attest, a project like this becomes all-consuming, not only for the student but for the spouse. So while most couples were having conversations about their day over dinner, we were more likely to talk about the construct of empathy. It even crept into our pillow talk late at night. Isn't that romantic?

In a strange sense, it actually is somewhat romantic. After all, mutual empathy has proven to be at the very core of what makes a couple click. So after all these years of studying empathy, what do we think it looks like?

That's where the "Trading Places Matrix" comes in. If you think about the two primary components of empathy—cognitive understanding (head) and emotional intuiting (heart)—and measure each of them along a continuum, you come up with the following diagram revealing four distinct styles.

The Four Social Styles

FEELING
Emotional Intuiting

	HIGH	LOW
THINKING Cognitive Understanding LOW	Sympathizer	Personalizer
HIGH	Empathizer	Analyzer

As you can see, the Trading Places Matrix gives us four inter-personal or *social styles.* It shows us that husbands and wives tend to sympathize, personalize, analyze, or empathize.

Of course nobody typically fits squarely and completely into any one of these single styles all the time. We routinely dip in and out of any of these quadrants, from moment to moment. A myriad of moods and the tenor of our day, not to mention our social setting, can all cause us to move into a particular mode—even one that is uncharacteristic of our usual social style. But generally speaking, most of us lean toward a relatively predictable pattern within these four quadrants. Here we want to take a closer look at each of them.

But before we do, we want you to be aware of an online tool that accompanies this book, something we think you'll find helpful.

Taking the Trading Places Inventory

If you're like most people, you may be wondering exactly where you tend to be, right now, in the Trading Places Matrix. What percentage of your social style, for example, is dominated by sympathizing or analyzing? If you'd like to find out, we offer a complimentary online assessment that will help you determine just that. The Trading Places Inventory (TPI) will take you just a few minutes, and it generates a personalized matrix based on a valid and reliable measure of your social style. It will also provide you with a brief report on your style and give you some specific suggestions as you move through the remaining chapters of this book. And you'll receive your results right on your computer (ready to print) as soon as you complete the questionnaire. Of course, the TPI is not required. It's simply an option that can augment your personal understanding and application of this material to your own marriage.

To take the TPI, simply go to www.RealRelationships.com and enter the code found on the inside of your book jacket. You'll also find a paper/pencil version of the inventory in the optional men's and women's workbooks that accompany this book.

Now, whether you have elected to take the free online TPI or not, let's take a closer look at the four primary social styles and how they apply to you and your marriage.

The Sympathizer
More Feeling than Thinking

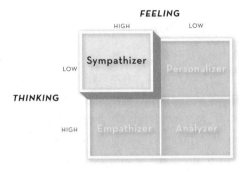

In the early days of aviation, pilots used a descriptive phrase, "Flying by the seat of your pants." Before instruments for aerial navigation were available, the only guide was the pilot's own sense of movement. If he felt pressure on the seat of his aircraft, it probably meant he was ascending, much the same as the feeling you get in a rising elevator. Conversely, if he felt weightless, the plane was probably descending. This method of flying, of course, was not at all reliable. Men died because their feelings played tricks on their judgment.

The same holds true in your marriage. Feelings can be just as deadly when they are the sole instrument for navigating your relationship. And if you're a hard-core sympathizer, you're probably blind to the danger. What you don't realize is that your sympathetic style causes you to jump to unfounded conclusions, which are based more on feelings than facts. You may see signs of disapproval from your partner where they don't exist. Or you will tend to project your own feelings onto your spouse before analyzing the situation to see if those feelings are accurate or not.

> When a good man is hurt, all who would be called good must suffer with him.
>
> Euripides

In a study of perception, researchers designed a split-screen viewing apparatus that could simultaneously flash two separate photos before one's eyes in a split second. For example, they showed at the same time a photo of a bullfighter and a photo of a baseball player. When they ran the experi-

32

ment in Spain, the subjects almost always reported seeing a bull-fighter. In America, subjects saw a baseball player.

The point? We all look at the world through the lens of our personal experiences and values. And when a Sympathizer looks at her husband, she often assumes her emotions are shared by him even when they aren't. The Sympathizer, like the pilot flying by the seat of his pants, needs to learn that her feelings can only go so far. Sound judgment and objective thinking are also required if she ever hopes to truly trade places in her marriage.

The good news? If you're a Sympathizer, you're halfway home to empathy and the joy of trading places. And this book will show you how to get there.

The Personalizer
Short on Both Feeling and Thinking

In one rendition of the classic fairy tale *Rapunzel* by the Brothers Grimm, a beautiful young girl is imprisoned in a tower by an old witch who insists that Rapunzel is ugly. One day when Rapunzel gazes from the window of her tower, she sees her Prince Charming standing below. He is enchanted by her beauty and tells her to let her long golden tresses down from the window. The prince then braids her hair into a ladder and climbs up to rescue her.

The implicit message of this fairy tale is simple and profound. Rapunzel's prison is really not the tower but her fear that she is ugly and unlovable. The mirroring eyes of her prince, however, tell her that she is loved, and thus she is set free from the tyranny of her own imagined worthlessness.

FEELING
HIGH   LOW

LOW   Sympathizer   **Personalizer**

THINKING

HIGH   Empathizer   Analyzer

The Personalizer is a bit like Rapunzel, imprisoned by fear. Whether it's because of cruel messages they received while growing up or from a previous marriage or some other brutal relationship, the Personalizer tends to suffer *from* people rather than *with* people. In other words, their social style causes them to withdraw and retreat in order to avoid potential pain. Because of this they have a tough time loving their spouse with their head or their heart. Their personal sensitivity to potential pain and rejection keeps them predominantly focused on themselves. It's what researchers call "affective blindsight."[3] Their lens of life is so distorted by previous pain that they can only rarely see life from their partner's point of view.

> Trying to observe the slow shift from self-centeredness to empathy is like trying to watch grass grow.
>
> **Neal Maxwell**

Mark Twain once said, "If a cat sits on a hot stove, that cat will never sit on a hot stove again." He continued, "That cat will never sit on a cold stove either." And if a Personalizer has been burned in a previous relationship, they don't want to get burned again. As they see it, the best way of avoiding potential pain is to guard their heart by keeping to themselves.

Unfortunately, that may even mean withdrawing from their spouse. Their own struggles are so heavy that they prevent them from entering their partner's. That's why it takes a special "prince" or "princess" to unlock the healing that will eventually get the Personalizer to a place where they can look at life through another's eyes and begin to practice empathy.

If you've been imprisoned by a painful past and you find yourself in the Personalizer category, we have a special message for you. We'd like you to turn to appendix B where you'll find some practical suggestions for learning to trade places. And if you are married to a Personalizer, we encourage you to turn to this appendix too.

The Analyzer
More Thinking than Feeling

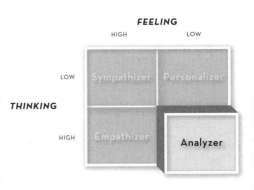

At a recent marriage retreat, the organizers asked that we divide the group by gender so that Leslie could meet with the women and I could meet with the men. Both of us agreed beforehand that we would ask our respective groups to describe a time they had helped their spouse with a problem by empathizing. We'd then ask those who felt especially good at helping their spouse solve problems through empathy to share what they do. Almost invariably, the answers we heard in each group involved exploring the other person's psychological state and explaining it to them in a kind of pop-psych approach.

Unfortunately, these well-intentioned spouses were not empathizing at all. They were psychologizing. They were saying things like, "You're projecting your own needs onto me and then trying to meet them to feel better about yourself." Or, "You probably feel neglected in this situation because it brings you back to being the youngest child in your family." To be honest, they were actually dismissing their spouse's problem by analyzing its supposed causes and cures. And psychologizing, no matter how well intended, is not empathizing. You see, empathy never imposes its own "diagnosis." It doesn't presume to know what's "really" going on. It merely attempts to accurately see the

> We do not know the inmost depths of the human heart; it is revealed only to love. But those who condemn have generally little love, and therefore the mystery of the heart which they judge is closed to them.
>
> **Nicolas Berdyaev**

situation from another's point of view. The Analyzer doesn't quite get that.

I (Les) should know. I've spent an embarrassing amount of time in my marriage psychologizing Leslie's "issues." Like a lot of husbands, I'm often quick to pull the problem-solving trigger before I even understand the problem. But, of course, this falls way short of empathy. Analyzing with your head and neglecting the importance of your heart will never move you to trade places.

So if this is where you tend to land on the Trading Places Matrix, take comfort in knowing that, like the Sympathizer, you already have half of what it takes to practice empathy. And we'll soon show you how you can gain what you're missing.

The Empathizer
A Good Measure of Both Thinking and Feeling

Of course, the most desirable place to be in the Trading Places Matrix is where analyzing and sympathizing converge. That's where true empathy resides. And, when you and your spouse move into this social style together, it will be the most important move the two of you will ever make.

It requires putting yourselves in each other's shoes with both your head and your heart. It requires a deep emotional attunement that is tempered by an objective cognitive capacity. In other words, it requires the head and the heart to moderate one other. That's the key.

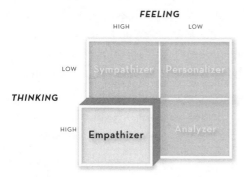

Not long ago, Jackson, our four-year-old, was watching Sesame Street when we noticed a familiar story. It was a takeoff on the famous

Brothers Grimm tale, *The Princess and the Frog*. As you know, the story typically ends with the spoiled princess kissing the frog, who becomes a prince. But in this Sesame Street version, Miss Piggy, adorned with her jeweled tiara, doesn't find her prince with a kiss. Instead, with her kiss she becomes a frog. Poof!

Jackson, like the program intended, laughed out loud. But it was John, our nine-year-old, who added a more serious observation: "If you want to know frogs, you've got to feel like a frog and think like a frog."

That's exactly what the empathizer does. He feels and thinks like his spouse. It's a tall order, no doubt. So if this isn't where you happen to be in the Trading Places Matrix, we're going to give you plenty of practical tools for getting there.

In fact, the remainder of this book is dedicated to helping you do just that.

> Yet, taught by time, my heart has learned to glow for others' good, and melt at others' woe.
>
> **Homer**

For Reflection

1. Do you agree that empathy is at the heart of love in your marriage? Why or why not?

2. What do you make of the Trading Places Matrix in this chapter? Does it clarify your own interpersonal style? How about your spouse's style? If so, how?

3. As you consider how to get better at trading places, what do you believe is going to be your biggest challenge and why?

Exercise One
Exploring Your Own Social Style

A brief note on our workbooks: Both you and your spouse can find this optional workbook exercise in the *Trading Places Workbook* (*for Men/for Women*). These exercises are not required — they are simply an additional resource if you'd like a tool to help you apply this content at a personal level. Workbooks are available separately at your local bookstore or online at www.RealRelationships.com.

Awareness is curative. We've said this countless times in our seminars across the country. Once you become aware of something about yourself, you can then do something about it. Of course, this chapter was intended to raise your level of self-awareness, but through this exercise we want to help you do something about your new understanding. We want to help you apply it in a personal way so that it can make a meaningful difference.

CHAPTER 2

What Trading Places Will Do for Your Marriage

*Empathy deploys a shorthand that gets two people
on the same page immediately,
without having to waste time or words
explaining what matters.*

Darryl McDaniels

We were sitting on an airplane when Les said, "Listen to this." He pulled down the tray from the back of the seat in front of him, and with wide eyes full of expectancy, began tapping on it with his index finger.

I listened for a moment, obviously puzzled. He just kept tapping and looking at me.

"Have you lost your mind?" I asked as I put my magazine down.

"I'm tapping a song. Can you guess what it is?" Les kept tapping as I only halfheartedly played along. "Come on, you can get this," he said.

That's when a curious passenger next to me, who had been completely quiet up to this point of the trip, piped up: "Is it Morse code?"

Les, suddenly self-conscious, stopped his tapping.

"Seriously, what's that all about?" I asked.

Les insisted it was a song and revealed that he'd been reading about a research project at Stanford University that compelled him to try the experiment on me.

The study was unusually simple. Elizabeth Newton, a doctoral student, assigned people to one of two roles: "tappers" or "listeners."[1] Tappers received a list of a couple dozen well-known songs, such as "Happy Birthday to You," "Mary Had a Little Lamb," and "The Star-Spangled Banner." Then, after selecting one of the songs, their task was to tap out the rhythm to a listener by knocking on a table. The listener's job was to decipher the rhythm being tapped and guess the song.

Pretty simple, right? Well, as it turns out, the listener's job is actually quite difficult—as the curious plane passenger and I soon discovered. Over the course of Newton's experiment, 120 songs were tapped out. Listeners guessed only 2.5 percent of the songs. That's just 3 correct guesses out of 120!

So what does this atypical doctoral dissertation have to do with trading places? Plenty. Here's what makes the results of Elizabeth Newton's study worthy of an advanced degree. Before the listeners guessed the name of the song, Newton asked the tappers to predict the odds of their listeners guessing correctly. The tappers predicted that their listeners would be right 50 percent of the time. In other words, tappers thought they were getting their message across one time in two. But, in fact, their message was only getting across one time in forty.

Why? Because when a tapper taps, she is *hearing* the song in her head. The tapping seems obvious to her. She can't help but hear it as she taps, and she therefore believes the listener has a very good chance of deciphering her tune. Try it yourself. Tap "Happy Birthday to You." It's impossible to avoid hearing the tune as you do so. And when your listener guesses, "Mary Had a Little Lamb," you wonder: *How could you be so stupid?*

Of course, the listener is not stupid. Not knowing what the tune is, he only hears a bunch of disconnected taps that resemble chicken pecks more than a musical number. But to the informed tapper, he comes off as dimwitted.

The same thing happens in marriage. When we "tap out" our message — whether it's with words, our inflection, or our body language — we believe it should be relatively obvious to our "listening" spouse. But it's not. Sometimes a seemingly evident message isn't evident at all. It's far from obvious if you're not in the know.

That's where the power of trading places comes in. Once you hone your empathic abilities, you will "tap" differently. What's more, you'll "listen" differently. In fact, when you harness the power of trading places in your marriage, you'll enjoy a connection with each other like you've never had before.

> A marriage where even one partner is very deficient in empathy is very unlikely to be a satisfying marriage. And a marriage wherein both parties have empathy in abundance is likely to be a very satisfying and happy one.
>
> **Bernard Guerney Jr.**

Of course, that's a pretty broad statement, so let's get specific. What exactly do you get when you enroll empathy in the service of your marriage? Plenty. We dedicate this chapter to showing you some of the most tangible rewards you'll reap from trading places. And at the end of the chapter, we will reveal a special bonus you're probably not expecting.

When you trade places in your marriage, here's what you get:

- You reduce critical comments.
- You eliminate nagging.
- You short-circuit conflict.
- You become better friends.

- You build a deeper commitment.
- You give and get grace more freely.
- You live longer and healthier lives.
- You help each other realize your dreams.

Sound too good to be true? It's not. Major research studies in recent years have revealed these rewards and many others to couples who practice mutual empathy. So let's take a closer look at each of these enviable assets that come to couples who trade places.

Trading Places
Curbs Your Criticism

Ever been inspired with an idea while taking a shower? That's what happened for Rev. Will Bowen. He became weary of hearing parishioners at his Kansas City church complain about everything from the temperature in the sanctuary to the choice of music on Sunday morning. So he did something drastic. He asked his flock to take a pledge: vowing not to complain, criticize, gossip, or use sarcasm for twenty-one days. Each person who agrees to taking this vow is issued a little purple bracelet as a reminder of their promise not to complain. If they find themselves complaining, they take off the bracelet, switch it to the opposite wrist, and start counting their complain-free days again.[2]

Pretty good idea, huh? After all, who wouldn't like to eliminate complaining—especially from their own marriage? Well, a little-known secret among marriage specialists is the fact that complaining is actually good for your marriage. You read that right! It's good for your marriage. Research at the University of Washington has shown that complaining, at a moderate level, helps couples air their grievances and keep improving. What isn't helpful to a marriage is *criticism*.

So what's the difference between criticism and complaining? Criticism almost always begins with *you* ("You always make us late!"), whereas complaining almost always begins with *I* ("I feel so frustrated when we are late to something that matters to me"). This may seem like a small matter of semantics, but it makes a big difference in your marriage.

> Everything that irritates us about others can lead us to an understanding of ourselves.
>
> **Carl Jung**

And when you practice trading places in your marriage, you automatically curb your criticism. You don't even have to wear a purple bracelet to do so; all you need to do is see your complaint from your partner's point of view. That's what converts an obnoxious criticism ("You never turn off the garage lights") to a more receptive complaint ("It bothers me when you don't turn off the garage lights").

Now you'll hear plenty of advice on how you shouldn't criticize your spouse. The question is how to quit. Well, trading places, as you'll see in an upcoming chapter, is your answer. It virtually eliminates criticism without you even trying.

Trading Places Eliminates Nagging

Nagging is criticism's close cousin. So while we're on the topic, we feel compelled to tell you that this bothersome behavior can also be extinguished through empathy.

Amy Sutherland learned this in an unlikely place, and she wrote about it for the *New York Times* in an article called, "What Shamu Taught Me About a Happy Marriage." Sutherland begins by explaining that after twelve years of marriage, she became dismayed that her husband Scott still exhibited several irritating habits. "These minor annoyances are not the stuff of separation and divorce," she writes, "but in sum they began to dull my love for Scott. So, like many wives before me, I ignored a library of advice books and set about improving him. By nagging, of course, which only made his behavior worse." She goes on to describe how her husband would drive faster instead of slower; shave less frequently, not more; and leave his smelly workout clothes on the bedroom floor longer than ever.

> If you treat your wife like a thoroughbred, you'll never end up with a nag.
>
> Zig Ziglar

The breakthrough came for Amy while re-searching a book. She attended a school for exotic animal trainers in California where she saw them teach dolphins to flip and elephants to paint. And that's when it clicked. She wasn't seeing the nagging from her husband's point of view. She wasn't thinking of how it would feel to be nagged.

So, she thought, if she were in her husband's shoes, she'd be far more motivated to improve her behaviors if she was rewarded for good rather than punished for bad. "After all," she reasoned, "you don't get a sea lion to balance a ball on the end of its nose by nagging."

Back in her home state of Maine, she began thanking Scott if he threw one dirty shirt into the hamper. "If he threw in two," she says, "I'd kiss him. Meanwhile, I would step over any soiled clothes on the floor without one sharp word, though I did sometimes kick them under the bed. But as he basked in my appreciation, the piles became smaller."[3]

Seeing her own nagging from her husband's point of view! That's empathy. And that's exactly what allows all of us to elimi-nate nagging from our own marriage.

Trading Places
Shortens Your Conflicts

There's an old joke about a couple, married for decades, living in a small town. Two elderly men are sitting on a bench and the one asks the other how Mr. and Mrs. Smith are doing. "You know how it is," comes the laconic reply. "They've only ever had one argument in their married life — and they're still having it."

Let's face it. Conflict is inevitable, even if it's the same fight over and over. But most of us don't limit our conflict to one area. After all, it takes very little for the fur to fly in most marriages. We end up arguing about silly little things: "Who took my pen?" Or "You just passed a parking space right there!" Such seemingly innocuous questions and statements, when augmented with a particular attitude, can ignite a major blowout. It's almost unavoidable. We can't eliminate conflict completely — not if we are being authentic with our feelings. But empathy can reduce conflict's lifespan and minimize its negative impact.

> Hot heads and cold hearts never solved anything.
> **Billy Graham**

How does empathy do this for us? By trading in the blame game for positive solutions. It exchanges "you" statements for "we" statements. A study reported in *Psychological Science* discovered that the "best" arguers are those who don't point their fingers. According to the study, the person who says "we" the most during an argument suggests the best solutions.

Researchers from the University of Pennsylvania and the University of North Carolina at Chapel Hill used statistical analysis to study fifty-nine couples. Spouses who used second-person pronouns (you) — as in "You always make us late" — tended toward negativity in interactions. Those making use of first-person plural pronouns (we) — as in "We're really running late" — provided positive solutions to problems.

The study concluded: "'We' users may have a sense of shared interest that sparks compromise and other ideas pleasing to both partners. 'You'-sayers, on the contrary, tend to criticize, disagree, justify, and otherwise team with negativity."[4]

In other words, when you trade places you make conflict inclusive. Empathy is the catalyst for inclusion. When times get tough, empathy propels us to say something like, "We sure are having a time of it" instead of, "You are making everything worse." Empathy eliminates finger-pointing, taking the focus off of a person to blame and moving it onto the problem to be solved. Like we said, it exchanges "you" statements for "we" statements.

Trading Places
Makes You Better Friends

"It is not a lack of love," said Friedrich Nietzsche, "but a lack of friendship that makes unhappy marriages." We tend to agree. And so do a lot of other social scientists. In fact, world-renowned marriage researcher John Gottman of the University of Washington told us one day over lunch: "Happy marriages are based on a deep friendship."

And get this, Gallup's research indicates that a couple's friendship quality could account for 70 percent of overall marital satisfaction.[5] In fact, the emotional intimacy a married couple shares is said to be five times more important than their physical intimacy. And, of course, your level of emotional intimacy has a lot to do with your physical intimacy. So, in a sense, if trading places can boost the quality of your friendship, that means it will, by default, ignite your love life too.

So how does empathy make you and your partner better friends? By helping you see something through his or her eyes for the first time. By helping you share something that, up until now, only your spouse has enjoyed. Consider Barbara Brown Taylor, a professor at Piedmont College in rural Georgia. She knows exactly how empathy can make you better friends. "My husband, Edward," Barbara writes, "is devoted to hawks and especially to the golden eagles that are returning to our part of Georgia. Driving down the highway with him can be a test of nerves as he cranes over the steering wheel to peer at the wing feathers of a particularly large bird." Her husband, like any bird enthusiast, wants to know, is it an eagle or just a turkey vulture? In fact, as Barbara says, Edward *has* to know, even if it means weaving down the road for a while, or running off it from time to time. "My view," she continues, "is a bit different: 'Keep your eyes on the road!' I yell at him. 'Who cares what it is? I'll buy you a bird book; I'll even buy you a bird — just watch where you're going.'"[6]

A couple of summers ago, Barbara and Edward's schedules kept them apart for two months and she thought she'd get a break from hawks. "Instead I began to see them everywhere," she says, "looping through the air, spiraling in rising thermals, hunkered down in the tops of trees. Seeing them, really seeing them for the first time in my life, I understood that I was not seeing them with my own eyes but with Edward's eyes. He was not there, so I was seeing them for him."

Barbara couldn't wait to connect with her husband and tell him of the hawks she'd seen. Why? Because Barbara experienced the fun of trading places with her husband. That's how empathy makes you better friends. Of course, it probably won't be empathizing with your spouse's love of hawks that brings you closer together. But it may be cooking, sports, architecture, computers, exercise, or something that you've never really given much consideration.

Trading Places
Bolsters Your Commitment

When Chris Spielman played for the Buffalo Bills, he was everything a middle linebacker should be: tough, strong, and smart, with passion, total commitment, and loyalty to the game. He played the entire 1995 season with a torn pectoral muscle that he sustained in the season opener.

But the game took a distant second place in his thinking during the 1998 season. He chose to stay home. He cooked, took care of his kids, and cared for his wife — by choice. Stephanie, Chris's wife, was struggling through the stark reality of breast cancer. Surgery, chemotherapy, and nausea were Stephanie's opponents. During her fight, Chris was at her side. Why? Because he couldn't imagine her going through this tough time without him. As he looked at her situation and imagined life from her angle, the decision was no longer even up for debate.

Asked by a reporter from the *Rochester Democrat and Chronicle* if he'd consider a return to the Bills late in the season, Spielman said, "I'd play in a heartbeat, but what kind of man would I be if I backed out on my word to her? I wouldn't be a man at all."[7]

> You will find as you look back upon your life that the moments when you have really lived are the moments when you have done things in the spirit of love.
>
> **Henry Drummond**

Truth is, it was more than his "word" that compelled Chris to make this decision. It was empathy. He chose to see life from Stephanie's perspective. And research shows that when a spouse makes practical decisions as a result of their marriage commitment, they generally do so out of a higher level of empathy. And these studies also reveal, not surprisingly, that these couples not only enjoy a deeper level of commitment as a result of empathy, but more satisfaction too.[8]

Football fans raved about Spielman's aggressive, leave-it-all-on-the-field style of play. But during the 1998 season, his wife was the only fan he cared about pleasing. In fact, when she lost her hair while undergoing cancer treatment, Chris shaved his own head in solidarity and in tangible support of her. By entering her world, Chris's commitment to Stephanie only grew stronger. Today, they are enjoying life with their two children, Madison and Noah, and are both active in raising funds for breast cancer research.

Trading Places Infuses Your Marriage with Grace

A rabbi taught that experiences of God can never be planned or achieved. "They are spontaneous moments of grace, almost accidental."

His student asked, "Rabbi, if God-realization is just accidental, why do we work so hard doing all these spiritual practices?"

The rabbi replied, "To be as accident-prone as possible."

The same is true of spontaneous moments of grace in marriage — those moments where we replace condemnation with undeserved love. You see, the more we practice empathy, the more likely grace is to infuse our relationship. And think what that would do for your marriage!

I've seen it firsthand. Not so long ago I (Leslie) did something that would have been catastrophically worse had it not been for a healthy dose of grace from Les. I was running errands in our car and since our youngest had fallen asleep in his car seat, I decided to drop him off back home with my husband so that my errands could go more quickly and so I wouldn't disturb Jack's slumber.

I'd pulled our car into our garage, opened the back door, struggled to finagle Jack out of his safety harness without waking him, and carried him upstairs. "Les," I told my husband who was working in his study, "I'm leaving Jack with you while I do some grocery shopping. He's asleep in his crib."

Les acknowledged my plan as I hurried back to the garage and jumped back into the car. But as I pulled out of the garage, a noise I'll describe as "unsettling" rang through our neighborhood. Turns out I'd forgotten to close the back door after taking little Jackson out of his car seat. So as I pulled out of the garage, the open door smacked the side of our garage and ripped the door clean off.

> When empathy speaks up, it takes away stupidity's microphone.
>
> **Anonymous**

Les flew down the stairs in an instant, wide-eyed, and saw me crying as I sat behind the wheel. The cause of this one-car accident was obvious. I gripped the wheel, bracing myself for what Les was about to say. But he didn't yell. He didn't lay blame. He kissed me on the cheek and said, "I was thinking we needed a new car door, so this is perfect."

Of course, I didn't deserve that kind of grace in that moment. My thoughtlessness not only cost us money, it meant we wouldn't be driving the next day on our long-awaited ski trip. But instead of guilt, condemnation, and anger, I got grace. Why? As Les said that evening over dinner, "If I were in your shoes in that moment, the last thing I would have needed from you was to be scolded."

You've heard the Native American proverb: "Do not judge your neighbor until you have walked two moons in his moccasins." Well, that certainly rings true when you practice mutual empathy. Because you've walked in each other's shoes, judgment is replaced by grace.

Trading Places
Will Help You Live Longer

If you're looking for a tangible reason to practice mutual empathy, look no further than the length of your life. It's true. Trading places will help you both live longer.

A marriage running low on empathy, research has shown, takes its biological toll on both partners. One study of happy newlyweds, still getting the hang of mutual empathy, found that a thirty minute confrontation about a disagreement caused the blood pressure of both partners to rise, and the indices of immune function (measured through six adrenal hormones) to be lowered for several hours.[9] And this was for happy couples!

Does the same hold true for older, more experienced couples? When similar studies were done on the endocrine and immune systems of couples married an average of forty-two years, the lack of empathy again spurred unhealthy declines in their bodies. And since aging weakens the immune and cardiovascular systems, tension and discord between older partners takes a greater toll on their health.[10]

On the other hand, couples who displayed empathy during their discussions reflected their relief in lower levels of the same hormones. The bottom line is that couples who trade places live healthier and longer lives. But there's more good news on the medical front for couples who trade places.

A 2005 study from researchers at Ohio State University showed that marital arguments and a lack of empathy have a negative impact on a spouse's recovering and healing process after an injury. The study looked at forty-two couples, all of which had been married for at least twelve years, during two clinical visits conducted two months apart. At the beginning of each visit, the researchers used a small suction device to inflict blisters on the arms of each participant. During the first visit, the spouses were lead in posi-tive discussions. For the second visit, however, the couples were encouraged to talk about things on which they disagreed. The sessions were videotaped to determine the degree of hostility be-tween each couple, and the wounds were monitored for blood flow and fluid accumulation. The study revealed that a thirty-minute marital disagreement adds a day or more to the healing process of a wound.[11]

One more study designed to assess the extent to which the people we love can lend us biological assistance when needed showed that spouses who could hold their partner's hand while experiencing pain during medical treatment, suffered far less anxiety. And when the scientists tried to measure whether it was holding anyone's hand or only a spouse's, they had to termi-nate that part of the study. Why? Because spouses always guessed correctly whether the hand was their spouse's or a stranger's.[12]

> True contentment comes with empathy.
>
> Tim Finn

So, trading places helps us not only live healthier and longer lives, it helps us cope better with physical pain and heal more quickly when we're injured. Not a bad health plan!

Trading Places
Gives Wings to Your Dreams

Had it not been for an empathic wife named Sophia, Nathaniel Hawthorne may not have been listed among the great names of American literature. When Nathaniel, a heartbroken man, went home to tell his wife that he was a failure and had been fired from his job as a weigher and gauger at the Boston Custom House, she made an exclamation of joy. "Now," she said triumphantly, "you can write your book!"

Nathaniel replied with puzzlement and a sagging confidence: "And what shall we live on while I am writing it?"

To his amazement, she opened a drawer and pulled out a substantial amount of money. "Where on earth did you get that?" he exclaimed.

"I have always known you were a man of genius," she told him. "I knew that someday you would write a masterpiece. So every week, out of the money you gave me for housekeeping, I saved a little bit. So here is enough to last us for one whole year."[13]

> I've learned that whenever I decide something with an open heart, I usually make the right decision.
>
> **Maya Angelou**

It was during that year that Nathaniel Hawthorne wrote one of the great novels in American literature, *The Scarlet Letter*.

Sophia believed in her husband Nathaniel because she entered his world. She knew his dreams and she understood his passion for writing. Empathy does that in a marriage. It helps us realize each other's dreams. You see, once you understand what energizes your spouse's vision for their life—as well as your life together—you're far more likely to do whatever you can to make those dreams a reality. And he or she is far more likely to do the same for you.

A Quick Recap

There you have it—eight of the most established benefits of trading places. As you practice mutual empathy, you'll create a well-coordinated duet of positive feelings.[14] In summary, when you trade places in your marriage, you'll achieve:

1. A reduction in critical comments.
2. The elimination of nagging.
3. A sure way to short-circuit conflict.

4. A means to becoming better friends.
5. The tools for developing a deeper commitment.
6. A sure way to give and get grace from each other.
7. The benefit of living longer and healthier lives.
8. A boost in realizing your dreams together.

Not bad, huh? But we have more good news. Reaping these rewards can come quicker than you think.

Don't believe us? Consider this: In the 1930s, American Airways, which later became American Airlines, had a tremendous problem with lost luggage. Passenger complaints kept coming even after the company tried their best to get their station managers to overcome the problem. Finally, LaMotte Cohn, general manager of the airline at the time, came up with an idea. Cohn asked all of the station managers from across the country to fly to company headquarters for a meeting. Then he made sure that every manager's luggage was lost in transit.

The result? You guessed it. The airline suddenly made a huge leap of progress in curtailing the problem of lost luggage. And it was all because the airline's personnel instantly saw the problem from their customer's point of view.[15]

When you accurately see any situation from another's point of view, when you can experience it like they do, you instantly take a different approach to it. We know that the word "instant" carries a strong promise, but it's true. Should we couch it by saying "almost instant"? We don't think so. Empathy can actually change everything in a moment. The moment you see a predicament from your spouse's angle, once you have put yourself thoroughly in his or her shoes, you change — that very instant.

Unlike the station managers for American Airways, you won't have to be goaded and pressured to make changes. You'll make the changes without further prodding. That's the promise of fast-acting empathy.

But maybe you need a little more convincing. Maybe you've been told that empathy takes too long. If so, allow us to underscore, before closing this chapter, just how quickly empathy can make a positive difference in your marriage.

Trading Places Works Fast

Some people argue that empathy is inefficient, that it takes too much time and effort. We couldn't disagree more. Empathy is highly pragmatic. It's the fastest way to make progress in your marriage. It saves you untold time in moving past difficulties, and it accelerates your success.

Think of any convoluted conversation you've ever had with your spouse. Maybe it was a misunderstanding about a prescription. Perhaps it involved misread motivations concerning a joke in front of friends. Or maybe it was a lack of appreciation that caused you to clam up. Whatever the problem, wouldn't you like a way to make it immediately disappear? Wouldn't you like a magic button that would suddenly make things better? Sure. Who wouldn't? Well, that's what trading places can do.

It's quick.

As you're about to see, empathy does not require a long, drawn-out conversation to get things back on track. It can literally happen in an instant. For example, Les and I recently had a conversation that became increasingly heated. It involved what to serve for a dinner party we were hosting in our home.

"You can just do enchiladas," Les asserted. "People love those."

"I'm not serving enchiladas," I protested. "These people are expecting a nice dinner."

"Well, then I don't know what to say," Les shrugged and left the room.

"Where are you going?" I shouted.

"I've got ice cream out on the counter in the kitchen," he hollered back.

I followed him into the kitchen and he could feel me gearing up for a hardheaded discourse on why enchiladas were not appropriate for the party and how he needed to be invested in this event as much as me.

Before we made it to the softening ice cream, Les turned to me, put his hands on my shoulders, and said, "Help me see this from your side."

That's all it took. In less than a minute I told him how I had a limited amount of time to choose a menu, make the food, get the house ready, arrange for child care, prep our second grader for a spelling test, take my mom to a doctor's appointment, and so on.

"No wonder you're feeling frazzled," Les confessed. "I didn't realize you had all that on your plate."

That was it. In a moment's time, Les suddenly saw my world from my perspective and the tension melted long before his ice cream. He offered to take a few of my tasks and we moved forward. The point is that without trading places, our enchilada exchange would have evolved into an emotional and time-consuming upheaval that neither of us wanted.

You get the point. So don't let anyone tell you empathy is time consuming. It's not. Nothing works faster than empathy!

By the way, studies in the medical field have underscored the efficiency of empathy. More and more doctors are learning its expedient value. Why? Because it impacts their bottom line. Physicians, of course, need to sense the anxiety and discomfort of their patients so they can treat them effectively. But they rarely "take the time" to do so. Believing it will slow them down, most physicians speed through their appointments without practicing much empathy. In fact, one study reveals that patients usually had an average of four questions in mind to ask, but during the visits they were able to ask just one or two. Once a patient started speaking, the first interruption by the physician occurred, on average, within eighteen seconds.[16]

Physicians who trade places with their patients, on the other hand, tell their patients what to expect from a treatment and they check in to be sure their patients understand what's happening. Incidentally, the lack of empathy is a primary predictor in malpractice lawsuits. And the time needed for a doctor to be successfully empathic? Just three minutes.[17]

We'll say it again, nothing works faster than empathy. And as we move forward in this book, you'll see exactly why that is. But in the next chapter, we want to let you know why some couples never reap the rewards we've talked about in this chapter. It's because they don't understand the prerequisite for trading places.

For Reflection

1. *As you consider the benefits of trading places for your marriage, which of the payoffs noted in this chapter excites you the most and why?*

2. *A common benefit of empathy is what some call an "infusion of grace" into your marriage. What would more grace and acceptance in your marriage do for the two of you?*

3. *What do you think about the point made in this chapter that says empathy works fast? That is, that empathy actually saves you time in the long run? Do you agree? Why or why not?*

Exercise Two
Getting What You Want

A common misnomer about empathy is that it is mostly for the person on the receiving end. In other words, people who aren't in the know don't realize that empathy is the fastest way for getting your own needs met too. This exercise will help you put into words exactly what you want most from your marriage and your spouse. In fact, it provides a veritable menu of potential items you'd like most. And, of course, it will help you increase the likelihood of getting exactly that.

CHAPTER 3

The Prerequisite for Trading Places

Empathy builds on self-awareness.

Daniel Goleman

"The boys' bedrooms are freezing," I snapped.

"I know, I'm trying to figure out this new thermostat," Les replied as he fiddled with the gizmo on the wall. We'd just moved into a new home after two years of planning and building.

"I liked our old thermostat where you just set the temperature and that was it," I said as Les was trying to figure out our new-fangled heating system.

"I understand, but this one's better," Les responded. "We're just going to need to figure it out."

"Well, I'm not having my boys sleep in those cold rooms tonight," I said. "They'll both wake up with pneumonia."

Les looked at me, as if to say, *Really? Don't you think you might be exaggerating just a bit?*

"I mean it," I continued, "this is crazy!"

"Leslie, take a deep breath," Les said in a calm but stern voice. "Nobody's getting pneumonia."

"It's like a freezer in there! Seriously!"

"I know," Les said. "That's why I'm working on it, but we've got to give it time to heat up."

"I don't even know why you had to have this fancy thing."

"What?! You think *I* had to have this?" Les asked. "We were both there when the guy said it worked great. You and I agreed on it."

"All I know is that my little boys' rooms are ice-cold." With that, I turned on my heel and walked away.

"Where are you going?"

"To find more blankets."

Truth is, those boys' rooms weren't nearly as chilly as our interaction. And why is that? Could it be that what I was *really* upset about was not the newfangled thermostat? Could it be that my emotions were running high because they were being fueled by another concern that wasn't being voiced?

Bingo!

Ever had one of these interactions? Silly question, I know. We all have conversations that seem to be more emotionally charged than necessary. We all have interactions that misstep and hiccup and turn sideways for reasons that aren't necessarily plain to see. They aren't technically "fights." They're just interpersonal rough spots — patches of the marital road that seem bumpier than the rest.

> Goodness consists not in the outward things we do but in the inward things we are.
>
> **Edwin Hubbel Chapin**

Not only that, every marriage has occasional off-kilter interactions that have seemingly nothing to do with the current verbal exchange. You know the feeling. It's when you are simply *off*. Out of sync. You feel like you're suddenly on different pages. You couldn't tell it if you read a transcript of the conversation between you and your partner, but you can feel it if you are in the room.

These unpleasant interactions, which pepper most marriages, are rarely explained by what's apparent on the surface. The cause — a realization which can remedy the situation and get you both back on the same page — is found at a deeper level. And it can always be rooted out by empathy, changing the interaction in an instant.

There's a catch, however. Empathy can never do its invaluable work unless it's predicated on emotional intelligence.

Are You Emotionally Intelligent?

In 1990 Yale psychologist Peter Salovey and the University of New Hampshire's John Mayer coined the phrase "emotional intelligence" to describe qualities that bring human interactions to their peak of performance. Harvard psychologist and *New York Times* science writer Daniel Goleman brought the phrase into the national conversation with his groundbreaking book *Emotional Intelligence*. He calls empathy our "social radar" and believes it operates at different levels. At the very least, empathy enables us to read another's emotions. And at the highest levels, empathy understands the concerns that lie behind the person's feelings.

The key to identifying and understanding your spouse's emotional terrain, experts agree, is an intimate familiarity with your own. Goleman cites the research of Robert Levenson at the University of California at Berkeley as a prime example. Levenson brings married couples into his physiology lab for two discussions: a neutral talk about their day and a second, fifteen-minute emotionally charged discussion concerning a disagreement.

Levenson records the husband's and wife's heart rate, muscle tension, changes

> Only as you know yourself can your brain serve you as a sharp and efficient tool.
>
> **Bernard M. Baruch**

in facial expressions, and so on. After the disagreement, one partner leaves. A replay of the talk is then narrated by the other partner, noting feelings on their end that were not expressed. Then the roles are reversed and that partner leaves, allowing the other person to narrate the same scene from their partner's perspective.

> Know thyself.
>
> Socrates

This is where researchers found something extraordinary. Partners adept at empathizing were seen to mimic their partner's body while they empathize. If the heart rate of the partner in the videotape went up, so did the heart rate of the partner who was empathizing; if the heart rate slowed down, so did that of the empathic spouse.

This phenomenon, called *entrainment*, demands we put aside our own emotional agendas for the time being to clearly receive the other person's signals.[1] For, as Goleman says, "When we are caught up in our own strong emotions, we are off on a different physiological vector, impervious to the more subtle cues that allow rapport."

The point is that if we don't know what we are feeling, we can't set our own emotions aside temporarily in order to enter the emotional world of our spouse. That's why emotional self-awareness is the prerequisite for trading places.

Opening the Door to Empathy

In our crabby conversation about the thermostat, the main issue for me was not the immediacy of getting my boys' rooms warmed up. Any sane person knows it will take awhile for a furnace to do its work. I also knew Les was working hard to improve the situation. That was obvious. And, yes, I was present and cast my favorable vote when we were deciding on our heating system. I had no right to blame Les for it. So why was I being so emotional? Why was I making my husband my adversary instead of my teammate?

I can tell you, now. And so can Les. The answer was found just beneath the surface of my outward emotions. In fact, as I was rummaging through our moving boxes to find our blankets, Les, very gently, came to me for a little emotional excavation.

"I wish we could put our hands on that Hudson Bay blanket we got in Calgary last year," he said.

I didn't respond.

"And I wish Jackson didn't have an ear infection," Les continued.

"I know," I piped up. "That's what's really concerning me."

"I know it is," Les said in a comforting voice. "Not to mention the fact that it's a week before Christmas and we don't have a tree, let alone groceries, and my parents are flying in tomorrow."

"Exactly," I said with relief (*he understands*). "This is the craziest timing ever."

"It's not a Norman Rockwell Christmas, that's for sure," Les quipped as he gently put his hands on my shoulders.

"Nope," I replied with a smile, "but if we're lucky, it might snow in our boys' rooms tonight."

"We can only hope," Les said deadpan, without missing a beat.

That was it. A brief moment of empathy from my husband turned our off-kilter mood around. Within a minute's time we were back on the same page, feeling connected.

Now I can almost hear you saying, "What moment of empathy?" Did you miss it? Were you expecting something more psychologically sophisticated? Empathy doesn't necessarily require anything more than letting your spouse know, with compassion, that you recognize what's going on inside of them. And that's exactly what Les did for me. Rather than trying to reason with me on the technicalities of how an HVAC system works, he revealed my true concerns about our family and Christmas in a caring tone. That's all it took to get me back on track.

But here's the thing. Les could have never done this if he was not aware of his own emotional terrain. He would have been unable to reflect back to me my concerns if he wasn't aware of feeling stressed out about the move himself. If he'd lacked emotional self-awareness in that moment, what would he have said instead?

Here are a few options that come to mind ...

"Do you realize how irrational and emotional you're being?"

"If you want to pick up the manual and figure this out yourself, be my guest."

"I'm happy to have this conversation when you're not being insane."

Take your pick. If you're like a lot of married couples, you probably already have. Most everyone is guilty of these kinds of caustic statements at one time or another, and Les could have certainly responded with one of them. And if he did, the result would have sent our emotions to yet another level of intensity and probably brought us into the realm of a true fight. Instead, he was self-aware enough to monitor his own uneasy feelings, and that served as a pathway to mine. In other words, his self-awareness allowed him to set his own emotional agenda aside and thus opened the door to empathy.

> Become aware of internal experiences so that it immediately becomes possible for a certain amount of control to be exerted over them.
>
> **Abraham Maslow**

I (Leslie) could also have defused the situation by doing my own emotional excavation. As soon as things got heated, I could have said, "I'm sorry, but I'm just so stressed about Jackson's ear infection, and Christmas coming, and your folks flying in. I just can't handle one more thing."

Thinking about
Our Feelings

At first glance, our feelings are rather obvious. If we asked you about your feelings during a particular interaction that you had earlier today, chances are you would quickly identify them: sad, guilty, excited, pleased, and so on.*

But if we're honest, more thoughtful reflection can remind us of times when we have been oblivious to what we really felt about something.[2] If you had a contentious conversation with your spouse last night that involved a misunderstanding about your in-laws (an easy target for emotional drama), for example, you might realize that what you expressed as anger at your spouse for not accepting your parents was really sorrow over not having the kind of relationship with them that you wanted your spouse to have.

> Emotions are good servants but bad masters.
>
> **Aesop**

Some say that our hearts hold dominion over our heads. In other words, without self-awareness, our emotions rule. We lack objectivity, and the emotional spillover of our conversations clouds our reason. "I was so angry," we say, "I couldn't think straight."

But not the person with emotional intelligence. They can explain the reasons behind the most unreasonable emotions. They can step back from their own emotional experience, insert a bit of objectivity, and manifest emotional self-awareness.

Psychologists call it *metamood*, meaning awareness of one's own emotions. Sociologists call it *self-observation*. Other's call it *mindfulness*. We prefer the term *self-awareness*. Whatever you call it, we're all talking about the attention we give to our internal emotional

---

* If you have difficulty identifying everyday feelings that may seem obvious to others, you may find appendix C helpful. It provides a simple plan for becoming more adept at identifying and articulating your own feelings.

state. And that attention requires objectivity,[3] or what some call a "second self." Novelist William Styron says, "A second self is able to watch with dispassionate curiosity as his companion struggles." And, thankfully, that kind of objectivity can be learned.

So if you're lacking emotional self-awareness, we dedicate this chapter to helping you make significant strides in that direction. We want to show you how to think more clearly about your feelings. Why? Because with emotional clarity comes a happier and healthier marriage.[4] We start with an eye-opening anatomy lesson.

The Anatomy of Your Emotions

Joseph LeDoux's parents owned a meat market in Louisiana. That's where Joseph learned about brains, cutting up cows' brains for sweetbreads. He was enamored by the folds and convolutions and patterns in the brain of a cow, especially the cerebellum. Well, to speed up the story, the butchers' son became a neuroscientist, and at New York University, he discovered the short-circuit in the brain that lets emotions drive action before the intellect gets a chance to intervene. This uncovering of brain pathways opened up a flood of new research.[5]

> Never lose your temper, except intentionally.
>
> **Dwight Eisenhower**

In the past decade or so, scientists have learned enough about the brain to make judgments about where, exactly, emotion comes from and why our feelings are so essential.[6] Primitive emotional responses, at one point, were the key to our survival: fear drives the blood into the large muscles, making it easier to run; surprise triggers the eyebrows to rise, allowing the eyes to widen their view and gather more information about an unexpected event. Disgust wrinkles up the face and closes the nostrils to keep out foul smells.

Emotional life grows out of an area of the brain called the limbic system, specifically the amygdala. That's where we experience delight and disgust and fear and anger. The neocortex enables humans to plan, learn, and remember. Lust grows from the limbic system; love, from the neocortex.

Animals like reptiles, which have no neocortex, cannot experience anything like maternal love; this is why poor baby snakes have to hide to avoid being eaten by their parents. Yikes! Fortunately, we humans, with our capacity for love, protect our offspring, allowing the brains of our young time to develop. The more connections between the limbic system and the neocortex, the more emotional responses are possible.

> The happiness of a man in this life does not consist in the absence but in the mastery of his passions.
>
> **Alfred Lord Tennyson**

Consider a hiker on a mountain path, for example, who sees a long, curved shape in the grass out of the corner of his eye. He leaps out of the way before he realizes it is only a stick that looks like a snake. Then he calms down; his cortex gets the message a few milliseconds after his amygdala and "regulates" its primitive response.

University of Iowa neurologist Antonio Damasio, author of *Descartes' Error: Emotion, Reason and the Human Brain*, worked with patients whose connection between their emotional brain (their limbic system) and neocortex had been severed because of damage to the brain. He discovered how central that hidden pathway is to how we humans live our lives. People who had lost that linkage were just as smart and quick to reason, but their lives often fell apart nonetheless. They could not make decisions because they didn't know how they felt about their choices. They couldn't react to warnings or anger in other people. If they made a mistake, like a bad investment, they felt no regret or shame and so were bound to repeat it.

If there is a cornerstone to emotional intelligence on which most other emotional skills depend, it is a sense of self-awareness, of being smart about what we feel.

Getting Smart about What You Feel

A person whose day starts badly at home may be grouchy all day at work without quite knowing why. Once an emotional response comes into awareness—or is physiologically processed through the neocortex—the chances of handling it appropriately improve.[7] This metamood or self-awareness is the ability to pull back and recognize that "what I'm feeling is anger," or sorrow, or shame.

We'll be honest—emotional self-awareness is not always easy. It's a difficult skill because emotions so often appear in disguise. If you are mourning the death of a friend, you will certainly be sad, but you may not recognize that you are also angry at your friend for dying—because this seems somehow inappropriate. If your child runs into the street, you're likely to yell and express your anger at his disobedience. But your anger may owe more to the fear you feel at what could have happened than it does to the disobedience.

> A fool gives full vent to his anger, but a wise man keeps himself under control.
>
> **Proverbs 29:11**

Like we said, emotional self-awareness can be a challenge. "Anyone can become angry —that is easy," wrote Aristotle. "But to be angry with the right person, to the right degree, at the right time, for the right purpose, and in the right way—this is not easy." He's right (as if Aristotle needs us to back up his point). Exercising control over one's emotions is not easy. But it can be done with the hard work of your will.

You see, you've got to *will* your awareness. You can't expect it to magically appear to you. You've got to decide — with intention — to be objective about your feelings. If you're not, you're likely to (1) be engulfed by your feelings, (2) suppress your feelings, or (3) resign to your feelings. Let us show you what we mean.

Some people become engulfed by their emotions

Some impulses seem to be easier to control than others. Anger, not surprisingly, is one of the hardest, perhaps because it primes us to action. Researchers believe anger usually arises out of a sense of being trespassed against — the belief that you are being robbed of what is rightfully yours. The body's first response is a surge of energy, the release of a cascade of neurotransmitters (called catecholamines). If a person is already under stress, the threshold for emotional release is lower, which helps explain why people's tempers flair during a hard day and become even more uncontrollable.

> When angry, count to ten before you speak; if very angry, a hundred.
>
> **Thomas Jefferson**

When we were in graduate school studying psychology, a popular view argued for letting your anger out. The idea was to have a good cathartic rant and thus emancipate your anger. Psychologists know better these days. Studies show that dwelling on anger actually increases its power. A far better approach is the old admonition of counting to ten. This allows your body a chance to process your adrenaline and get some distance from this red-hot emotion.

Of course, people become engulfed by more than anger. We've all seen people that are emotionally out of control or unstable.

They give into whatever emotional wave rolls up on their psyche — whether it be sadness, anxiety, or surprise. They feel helpless in managing their emotions and allow their moods to take charge. Rather than having a bit of objectivity that might allow them to alter their moods, they do little to cultivate self-awareness, and as a result, feel overwhelmed.

Some people try to suppress their feelings

Two complete strangers had just watched a tormenting World War II documentary on the human suffering in the aftermath of the bombing of Hiroshima. Both felt deeply disturbed by what they had seen. But when they started talking together about their feelings, something strange happened. One of them was up-front and candid about feeling upset and saddened. The other person seemed indifferent, almost emotionless — which was exactly the point.

> The greatest of faults ... is to be conscious of none.
>
> **Thomas Carlyle**

These two strangers were volunteers in an experiment at Stanford University on the social consequences of suppressing your emotions.[8] While plenty of research has been done on the internal consequences of stuffing one's feelings, little had been studied on how this act impacts other people. Turns out the second person had been instructed to hide her true feelings. Understandably, the person who was open with her emotions felt out of sync and out of kilter with her cohort. And not surprisingly, she felt little or no warmth toward her.

That's the consequence of being with someone who keeps their emotions hidden. Of course, you probably didn't need a scientific study to tell you that. We've all experienced the awkward and disquieting experience of being with someone who sits on their feelings. And some misguided folks mistake emotional self-awareness with emotional suppression. Don't make that mistake. It's a practice that's made psychoanalysts rich.

Willing your awareness of your emotions has nothing to do with repressing them. Quite the opposite; as you become aware of your emotions, you don't stomp them out, you manage them — to keep them working for you rather than against you. In other words, emotional self-awareness gives you control over your feelings.

Some people resign to their feelings

Unlike those who are engulfed by emotions, these individuals clearly know what they are feeling. However, they do little to try and manage their emotions. Take worry as an example. While not the most productive of emotions, it is certainly not all negative. At its best, worry helps us rehearse for danger. The act of fretting focuses our mind on a problem so we can search more efficiently for solutions.

The problem arises when worrying blocks our thinking, becoming an end in itself or a path to resignation instead of perseverance. When that happens, we simply give in and let our worry take control. The result? Overworrying about a potential failure actually increases the likelihood of that failure. A salesman, for example, can resign himself to fretting about his declining sales, so much so that he can't bring himself to pick up the phone and attempt another. His resignation to worry guarantees that his sales will fall even further.

> An anxious heart weighs a man down.
> **Proverbs 12:25**

Despite clarity about their moods, people who resign to their feelings don't recognize the power they have to alter them. If they feel depressed, for example, they may recognize and talk about their sad feelings, but they do nothing to change them despite their distress. Of course, it doesn't have to be that way. Numerous studies have shown the power we have to change our moods. But, as you might guess by now, it begins with the *will* to do so.

Okay. So emotional self-awareness can be a challenge. We know that exercising control over our emotions is not always easy. But it becomes easier than we think once we conjure up the will to do so, once we become *intentional* about our objectivity.

That's when we're struck with a realization. We realize we don't have to be engulfed by our feelings. We don't have to suppress our feelings. And we don't have to resign to our feelings. No. With a little intentional thinking, we can become emotionally self-aware and effectively manage our emotions.[9]

The Realization

"This is anger I'm feeling." That simple self-statement, never uttered aloud, opens the door to freedom. How? It gives you the option not to act on it. It gives you the option to keep it alive or to tone it down.

> *Knowing thyself is a way of making thyself as palatable as possible to others.*
>
> **Steven Pinker**

Once an emotional response like anger comes into your awareness — once you pull back and acknowledge what you're feeling — the chances of using that emotion to your advantage greatly improve. In fact, through emotional self-awareness, your emotions become tools in your hands, allowing you to craft empathic interactions that would have otherwise been lost. Think of the monumental moments missed across the ages by couples who were out of sync because their emotions ruled their relationship. And if you dare, think of the emotional moments in your own marriage that left both of you feeling detached because neither one of you tuned into your own feelings and stepped outside yourself.

It's not a happy thought. But here's the good news. The sooner you become intentional about tuning into your own emotions as you interact together, the sooner you will experience the realization that you can monitor and manage your own emotions. This realization means you can control an impulse to lash out at your spouse. It means you can put off immediate gratification for yourself in order to soothe your partner's spirit. It means you can regulate your moods and create a more positive atmosphere together. Most of all, by becoming aware of your own emotional terrain, you will become able to set aside your own emotional agenda so that you can walk in your spouse's shoes. And that realization changes everything.

It's Your Choice

In 1997, when Oprah Winfrey was preparing to play Sethe in the movie *Beloved*, she arranged a trip along a portion of the Underground Railroad. "I wanted to connect with what it felt like to be a slave wandering through the woods," she said, "making the way north to a life beyond slavery—a life where being free, at its most basic level, meant not having a master telling you what to do every minute." To immerse herself in the experience, Oprah was blindfolded and taken into the woods where she was left alone to contemplate how she would find her way to the next safe house. "I understood for the first time that freedom isn't about not having a master. Freedom is about having a choice."[10]

> Clarity of mind means clarity of passion, too; this is why a great and clear mind loves ardently and sees distinctly what it loves.
>
> **Blaise Pascal**

The freedom to choose. That's the kind of freedom emotional self-awareness brings. Every emotion offers a choice. And every feeling has value. It can teach us something about ourselves. So the last thing we want to do in the process of trading places is to ignore our emotions. But we do want to have a say in how long an emotion will last or how intense it can get.

To the degree that our emotions get in the way of or enhance our ability to think and plan, to pursue a goal, or solve a problem, they define our capacity to love our spouse. In other words, our ability to manage our own emotions will determine our capacity to trade places.

Regardless of your motivation, if you lack the awareness of your own emotions, you will lack the aptitude for empathy. You may possess the *will*, but you're lacking the *way*. Emotional self-awareness is the path to seeing life from your partner's point of view.

For Reflection

1. *The premise of this chapter is that your ability to manage your own emotions determines your capacity to trade places. Do you agree? Why or why not?*

2. *Would you say that you are most likely to be engulfed by your feelings, to suppress your feelings, or to resign to your feelings? Why?*

3. *Assuming that you agree with the idea that you decide — with intention — to be objective about your feelings, how and when are you best able to do this personally?*

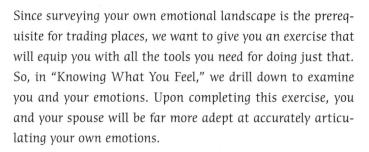

Exercise Three
Knowing What You Feel

Since surveying your own emotional landscape is the prerequisite for trading places, we want to give you an exercise that will equip you with all the tools you need for doing just that. So, in "Knowing What You Feel," we drill down to examine you and your emotions. Upon completing this exercise, you and your spouse will be far more adept at accurately articulating your own emotions.

PART TWO

THREE CRUCIAL STEPS TO TRADING PLACES

Did you know you can improve a second grade teacher's effectiveness by having her walk through her classroom on her knees? As she sees that space from a second grader's perspective, she will naturally be better equipped to teach her little pupils.

Any profession can be improved with more empathy. Did you know that the major fast food chains spend bundles of money sending "fake customers" into their stores to see the experience through the customer's eyes? Advertising firms on Madison Avenue make their living by putting themselves in the consumer's shoes.

Growing churches are growing because they study the experience of a first-time visitor and the pastor imagines what it is like to sit in the pew. Disneyland's "cast members" know that guests will average sixty contact opportunities in a single day at their theme park, and they want to make each of them a magic moment, so they continually work at empathizing with families.[1] Of course, a counselor wouldn't last a day without practicing empathy.

The question is how? How do they empathize? How does *anyone* empathize — especially in marriage?

Here's our answer:

* Step #1: Set Aside Your Own Agenda (Temporarily)
* Step #2: Turn on Your Emotional Radar
* Step #3: Demonstrate Your Care and Concern

These three steps are designed to be practical.

Now, normally, we would cringe at the thought of taking such a complex and intricate human process as empathy and breaking it into a seemingly trite three-step process. But, in fact, the research is clear. If you want to accurately empathize with your spouse, it really is almost as easy as $1-2-3$.

Here's the sequence in short:

> I notice you,
>
> I feel with you, and so
>
> I act to help you.[2]

In this section of the book, we take a close and careful look at each of these three steps and show you, in very practical terms, how to put them into practice.

CHAPTER 4

I Notice You
Setting Aside Your Own Agenda (Temporarily)

Love your neighbor as yourself.
Matthew 19:19

Angela teetered as she walked across a medical conference room, thighs chafing, sweat glands working overtime. She tried to squeeze into a regular-sized chair, but her lumpy hips snagged on the arms. She moved to an extra-wide armless chair, but then she couldn't cross her plumped-out legs.

A dietitian helped her climb aboard a stationary bicycle that had been fitted with an oversized seat. But when Angela tried to pedal, thick, doughy rolls of abdominal tissue pressed against her fleshy thighs, impeding movement.

"Every move I made was an effort," Angela, thirty-five, later admitted. By then, however, she had taken off her "fat suit" and had slimmed down to her actual weight of 130 pounds.

Angela had been zipped into a bulky, beige "empathy suit" designed to help medical personnel better understand the plight of their obese patients. The suit effectively blimps out small, low-fat people like Angela. Its sheer heft and bulk is intended to give them a new, deepened understanding of the workaday world of the obese.[1]

Does it work? You bet. Angela saw firsthand that even a simple movement such as walking may be challenging for the obese. Having worn the suit "makes me feel more respectful, more aware of their feelings," she says. "I literally forgot about myself and became another person."

That's the power of walking in another's shoes. And it happens only when you set aside your own agenda. For a physician like Angela, that means setting aside her need to treat a *patient*, and instead, treating a *person*. By putting her medical to-do list on hold, she enters another person's experience and offers more effective help.

This practice is more common than you might guess. Have you ever heard of the "pregnancy simulator"? It lets a soon-to-be father know what his wife is going through as she carries their baby. Through the use of a rib belt and strategic positioning of various weighted components, the garment enables him to experience many of the common symptoms and effects of pregnancy, including weight gain, fetal kicking, shallow breathing, and so on.[2] The effect on husbands is remarkable. They show greater patience and understanding of their wife's pregnancy experience. While wearing the simulator, they can't help but to go outside themselves and see the experience differently.

> Man's capacity to experience himself as both subject and object at the same time is necessary for gratifying living.
>
> **Rollo May**

And that's the key. Before we enter our partner's experience, we have to first *go* outside our own. We have to make a psychological move beyond our preoccupation with our own interests and desires. Of course, that's not our normal focus, as we're about to demonstrate.

A Personal Revolution

In the three-step process of trading places, the first step refers to going outside yourself. This often grates on our very nature. Why? Because most of the time we wander around this planet wishing people were more like us. *If my boss would just see things from my angle, he'd want to promote me. If people on this freeway would drive more like me, it would be so much easier. And if this person I'm married to would just do things the way I want them done, we'd have a great marriage.* Of course, we don't normally articulate such self-centered thoughts, but much of the time, that's what is going on at some level in our minds.

> If you live only for yourself, you are always in immediate danger of being bored to death with the repetition of your own views and interests.
>
> **W. Beran Wolfe**

Like we said, it's our nature—from the very beginning. Little Suzy, for example, gets a phone call from her father, who asks little Suzy if Mommy is home. Instead of saying yes, little Suzy nods her head. Her father, hearing no response, asks again, to which little Suzy again nods her head. What little Suzy fails to appreciate is that her father is unable to see her nodding. Little Suzy can only take her own perspective—"I am nodding my head yes; why do you keep asking me this question?"

This self-referent perspective we have as three-year-olds, of course, matures. We eventually learn to go outside ourselves and reference another person's perspective. But the basic inclination to see the world from only our view stays with us. Even as adults we become puzzled that another person doesn't see, hear, or understand the way we do. Remember the music tapping study at Stanford that we talked about in chapter 2? It's a perfect illustration of this fact.[3] Like little Suzy, we just don't understand why the listener can't decipher our taps to pick up on the tune we have in our head.

Historically, this kind of self-centered thinking even happened on a global level. Five hundred years ago we thought the earth was the center of the universe. And when Copernicus proposed a different perspective, that the earth was one of many planets rotating around the sun, the idea was truly revolutionary. And you'll experience a personal revolution in your own marriage every time you move beyond the concerns of your self-focused agenda to recognize your spouse's perspective.

A Quick
but Important Point

Now, before we go much further in this chapter, we want to clear up any potential for misunderstanding. Did you notice the parenthetical word in this chapter's title: *Temporarily.* This chapter is not asking you to *permanently* set aside your own agenda. We're not asking you to bury your own needs and forget about them. Not at all. In fact, it's vitally important that you keep your personal agenda close at hand, as you'll soon see.

> Being part of an agenda beyond ourselves liberates us to complement each other rather than compete with each other.
>
> **Joseph Stowell**

So know this: Mutual empathy doesn't ask you to go without getting your needs met. Trading places does not mean your agenda will always take a back seat. Once you experience mutual empathy you'll soon see how your own needs are getting met like never before. Why? Because when your spouse feels validated and understood, he or she feels compelled to do the same for you. That's what sends a couple's marital satisfaction through the roof.

Do You See What I See?

The person who is unwilling to set aside his own agenda is like a person who is wearing mirrored sunglasses with the lenses flipped around. As he looks out at the world, all he can see is a reflection of his own needs and desires. It's called *egocentrism* — the well-established social psychological phenomenon whereby people have a difficult time detaching themselves from their own perspectives. It can take a variety of forms.[4]

- *Egocentric memory* is our tendency to "forget" evidence and information which does not support our thinking. Instead, we "remember" evidence and information which supports our stance.

- *Egocentric infallibility* is our tendency to think that our beliefs are true because we believe them. We wouldn't hold a position that isn't right, we say to ourselves, so the position we are currently holding *has* to be right.

- *Egocentric righteousness* is the tendency to feel superior in light of our confidence that we are in possession of the truth. You see this demonstrated plainly on talk shows where political agendas are debated.

All of these forms have one thing in common: None of them allow for a listening ear. They're only concerned about pushing their own perspective. They shut down any possibility of listening intently. In other words, they prevent you from going outside your own agenda.

Wouldn't it be helpful to have an empathy suit for your marriage? Can you imagine slipping on a garment that would ensure you'd temporarily set aside your own agenda and listen intently as you more accurately understand your spouse's thoughts, feelings, and actions? Think of it. You could come home from work, even if you're exhausted, put on an empathy suit—both of you—for about ten minutes or so as you debrief your day together. How would that impact your marriage? At the very least it would set the tone for an evening where you felt completely understood and completely understanding. You'd both feel connected and in sync. Think how it would impact your level of intimacy, not to mention your love life!

> Lovemaking is, at its best, an act of mutual empathy.
>
> **Daniel Goleman**

Well, in a sense, you can put on an empathy suit. Both of you can slip into your partner's world routinely. All you have to do is learn the secrets to setting your personal agenda aside—temporarily.

So let's take a look at the five secrets to setting aside your own personal agenda.

Secret #1
Know Your Own Agenda

To set aside your agenda, you have to know what your agenda is. Self-awareness, as you recall, is a prerequisite to empathy. Your agenda is nothing more than your set of immediate goals. That includes what you want to do (finish this chapter, decide on dinner plans, take a walk), what you want to feel (enlightened, challenged, superior), and what you want to talk about (a vacation, a challenge at work, how you felt hurt last night).

Your personal agenda is continually updated and revised. And it's a powerful force. It compels you to keep focused on your goal. Like an executive running a high-powered board meeting, you don't want to veer away from your agenda because it means you may not reach your goal. The difference, of course, is that your agenda is not printed for distribution to family and friends. Sometimes your agenda remains unspoken. Sometimes, nobody knows it but you.[5]

On the other hand, your agenda is often straightforward and out in the open. It may be an intensely emotional message you want to get across. It's not disguised or cloaked in mystery. You, for example, may want your spouse to know you're angry. You may want your spouse to know that you won't stand for being belittled in front of your friends. And what happened earlier in the evening is something you don't want to ever happen again. In fact, you want your spouse to pay a price for having embarrassed you. So what do you do? You raise your voice, you pace around the room, you point your finger, and you induce guilt. Or maybe you clam up and retreat to another part of the house in an attempt to get your message through and punish your partner. The point is, you will do whatever you can to accomplish your agenda. And the last thing you want to do when your agenda is red-hot is set it aside. In fact, in those moments when your amygdala has been hijacked, it is nearly impossible to do so.

> Nothing said to us reaches us so deep as that which we find in ourselves.
>
> **Theodor Reik**

But your agenda doesn't have to be an intense and emotional message you want to get across. It may just involve talking on your cell phone. Let's face it, our full attention has become endangered in this age of multitasking. It becomes blunted whenever we split our focus. "A five-minute conversation can be a perfectly meaningful human moment," an article in the *Harvard Business Review* notes. "To make it work, you have to set aside what you are doing, put down the memo you were reading, disengage from your laptop, abandon your daydream, and focus on the person you're with."[6]

Wherever your personal agenda item falls on the continuum from hot to cold, you'll have to know what it is in order to set it aside.

Secret #2
Practice Priming

Most people don't know that you can orient your psychological circuits for connection. Scientists call it *priming*. Simply thinking of an action prepares the mind to perform it. If you think about how you will greet a person you're meeting for lunch, if you give a moment's thought to them and what their life is about, your initial greeting as well as your conversation will be warmer. You'll feel more connected and in tune.

The same applies to your marriage and trading places. You can prime yourself for seeing your partner's perspective. If you give a moment's thought to setting aside your own agenda when you see your spouse at the end of the day, you'll probably do so with ease. Think this through. As you pull into your garage, if you take just ten seconds to consider what your spouse has been doing and how they may be feeling, you'll make a connection that is not all about you. Compare that to the mind-set that results from arriving home after a day of work and thinking that you need to call a friend, catch up on email, or maybe just kick your shoes off and enjoy something cold to drink. Of course, there is nothing wrong with these thoughts. But they do precious little to prime you for considering anyone else's agenda but your own.

> Goodness consists not in the outward things we do but in the inward things we are.
>
> **Edwin Hubbel Chapin**

Does this make sense? Priming can seem so insignificant, so elementary, that its profoundness can be lost. The best way to realize its power, of course, is to try it. Prime your mind before you connect with your spouse. Take just a few seconds to consider what your spouse's experience is like. One of the ways we put priming into practice is by asking a simple question: How would I be feeling and what would I be thinking if I were in my partner's shoes?

That's all it takes to trigger priming. And don't think you can only prime yourself for empathy upon meeting at the end of your workday. You can ask yourself this question at any time, even if you're already together. Ask the question to yourself while you're having dinner, watching television, or getting ready for bed. Priming works at any time and any place. Thinking of an action always prepares the mind to perform it.

Secret #3
Offer an "Agendaless" Presence

Most couples never understand this invaluable secret: When you empty yourself of your need to change another person, the things that irritate you about them have the opportunity to become the things that endear you to them.

Two weeks into our marriage we were in our new little kitchen making a salad together. Leslie, who is left-handed, was cutting carrots.

"What are you doing?" I asked.

"Cutting the carrots," was her sensible reply.

"You're going to kill yourself—holding the knife like that."

That's when I proceeded to give Leslie a lesson in the way I thought she should cut carrots. Did it work? Not for long. The next time she cut carrots it was the same way she had before.

"Leslie, how many times do we have to cover this?" I asked.

"Oh, I forgot," she replied, as she went back to my way of cutting carrots.

How many times do you think we've had this conversation over the past two decades of our marriage? Countless times. And how

> The language of your spouse may be as different as Chinese from English. We must be willing to learn our spouse's primary love language if we are to be effective communicators of love.
>
> **Gary Chapman**

do you think she cuts carrots today? That's right. The same way she always has.

But here's the strange thing. A few years ago, while watching Leslie cut carrots as I was listening to voice mail on our phone in the kitchen, I realized something. I'd be disappointed if she were cutting carrots any other way.

Can you believe that? After all these years of trying to convert her to my way of cutting carrots, I realized that I liked the way she cut them. Why? Because that's the way "my Leslie" cuts carrots. I'm sure this seems strange, but somewhere along the way in our relationship I emptied myself of my need to change the way she cuts carrots, and now I found it endearing.

That's the payoff of being present without an agenda. You see, an agendaless presence allows our partner to be who they are — to simply relax in our presence. But it also allows us to take a deep breath and not be so uptight about having everything go our way.

An agendaless presence begins when you empty yourself of your compulsive need to change your spouse's behavior, thinking, attitude, or emotion. It emerges when you offer undivided attention coupled with sustained presence. Wouldn't you like to receive this from your spouse from time to time? This is a gift that benefits the giver as well. Try it. You'll be amazed by the benefits that come back to you.

Secret #4
Move from "It" to "You"

We all want emotional closeness in our marriage. We want to experience a strong connection and a deep bond. And we know this can only happen when we are wise enough, on occasion, to step back from our own agenda and concentrate on our partner's. And one of the best ways of doing just that is to move from "it" to "you."

That's the way Austrian-born philosopher Martin Buber put it in his classic book *I and Thou*. First published in 1923 and eventually translated into numerous languages, the book introduced the concept of *dialogue*, where you suspend your pre-established opinions and judgments, allowing another person's opinions and judgments to be fully expressed.[7]

In what he called an "I-it" interaction, you are looking down on another person and the situation is void of a full emotional connection. In fact, it feels hollow because we're treating the other person as an object instead of a person. Contemporary psychologists use the term "agentic" for this cold approach to others, viewing people as a means to help us reach our own goals. A person is agentic when they don't care at all about your feelings, but only about what they want from you. This egocentric behavior epitomizes the person that can't let go of their own agenda.

> Effective listening requires more than hearing the words transmitted. It demands that you find meaning and understanding in what is being said. After all, meanings are not in words, but in people.
>
> **Herb Cohen**

In contrast, Buber described the "I-You" interaction as a kind of "communion" where another's feelings are validated, perused, and understood. In this interaction, another person's feelings do more than matter; they change you.

One of our single friends used to employ a test on every first date. She would count the amount of time it would take before her date asked her a question with the word "you" in it. In other words, she was looking for her date's capacity to tune into her world. Not surprisingly, she married a man who barely gave her time to start the clock. He knew how to cultivate an I-You relationship.

The I-You relationship, as Buber put it, "can only be spoken with the whole being."[8] It requires more than lip service. A defining quality of I-You is "feeling felt." It's the sensation of having someone get inside your feelings with you. It's the knowledge that they have stepped out of their own agenda to enter yours. The I-You transaction is one of the great secrets to building a strong connection and a deep bond.

Secret #5
Listen with the Third Ear

The final secret we want to impart here is probably the most well-known. If you want to move outside your own agenda, you've got to listen aggressively.

At the university where we teach, a new vice president for campus life showed up at our departmental meeting. Surely he's in the wrong place, we thought, or maybe he came to make an announcement or make a quick introduction and run. Nope. Turned out that he was there to listen. He had no agenda other than that. "I'm spending the first few weeks on the job just listening," he told us. He attended a meeting of nearly every group on campus in his first two months and didn't utter a peep of advice. True to his word, he just listened. The result? He became one of the most well-liked leaders on our campus in years.

Listening, where the listener checks with the speaker to see that a statement has been correctly heard and understood, is one of the fail-safe ways for building an interpersonal bridge. And it's a skill we take for granted in marriage, primarily because we confuse good listening with hearing words. But as Peter Drucker put it, "The most important thing in communication is to hear what isn't being said."

That's the secret of listening with the "third ear." Psychoanalyst Theodor Reik used this phrase to describe the action of hearing more than just words. Whenever you hear your spouse speak, there is a river of emotions that flows between you. And when you listen with the third ear, you not only hear the verbiage in your dialogue, but you are dipping down into that river of emotions to reflect the feelings you find back to your partner.

> The biggest mistake you can make in trying to talk convincingly is to put your highest priority on expressing your ideas and feelings. What people really want is to be listened to, respected, and understood.
>
> **David Burns**

Consider this example: A wife walks into the family room and says to her husband, "I feel like such a failure when this place isn't picked up and I know your mom is dropping by tomorrow."

Pretty straightforward, right? He heard her words. Well, what is she saying exactly? It may not be what you think. Consider a few different ways this brief exchange could go:

Husband: Sounds like you think the house is a mess.
    Wife: Oh, no. It's always going to be like this until the boys are older.

or

Husband: You sound a little depressed; are you alright?
    Wife: I'm not depressed; I think I'm mostly upset that my boss wouldn't give me tomorrow off.

or

Husband: Is my mom's visit stressing you out?
Wife: Actually, I'm thrilled that she'll be here. I just wish
I had the energy to vacuum tonight.

See how it works? A simple inquiry to make sure you understand what isn't being said goes a long way in helping you set your personal agenda aside. Listening with the third ear keeps you from jumping to conclusions. When you set aside your own agenda, you listen with full receptivity and dig a little deeper into the conversation to make sure you understand.

You'll Never Take the First Step of Empathy If You Don't Have This

The Jewish poet and storyteller Noah ben Shea tells a parable that serves as a valuable reminder of this first act of trading places. After a meal, some children turned to their father, Jacob, and asked if he would tell them a story. "A story about what?" asked Jacob.

"About a giant," squealed the children.

Jacob smiled, leaned against the warm stones at the side of the fireplace, and his voice turned softly inward. "Once there was a boy who asked his father to take him to see the great parade that passed through the village. The father, remembering the parade from when he was a boy, quickly agreed, and the next morning the boy and his father set out together. As they approached the parade route, people started to push in from all sides, and the crowd grew thick. When the people along the way became almost a wall, the father lifted his son and placed him on his shoulders."

> We've all heard the criticism "he talks too much." When was the last time you heard someone criticized for listening too much?
>
> **Norm Augustine**

"What happened next?" a little boy asked Jacob.

"Soon the parade began and as it passed, the boy kept telling his father how wonderful it was and how spectacular were the colors and images. The boy, in fact, grew so prideful of what he saw that he mocked those who saw less, saying, even to his father, 'If only you could see what I see.'

"But," said Jacob staring straight in the faces of the children, "what the boy did not look at was why he could see. What the boy forgot was that once his father, too, could see."

Then, as if he had finished the story, Jacob stopped speaking.

"Is that it?" said a disappointed girl. "We thought you were going to tell us a story about a giant."

"But I did," said Jacob. "I told you a story about a boy who could have been a giant."

"How?" asked the children.

"A giant," said Jacob, "is anyone who remembers we are all sitting on someone else's shoulders."

"And what does it make us if we don't remember?" asked the boy.

"A burden," answered Jacob.[9]

This is the ultimate secret to the first step in trading places: remembering that we are sitting on someone else's shoulders. The moment we begin to think that we have gotten to where we are solely by our own efforts, we stomp out humility. Arrogance enters the picture. And know this: arrogance always breeds conceit and callousness. Any act of love done from a callous heart is done for show. It is void of authenticity. It may be the right thing, but it is done for all the wrong reasons.

A kind and compassionate heart is found in the husband or wife who may be well accomplished, wildly successful, immensely powerful, but who is also humble. Humility is the ultimate secret to setting aside your own agenda. It opens the door and makes a way for empathy. As William Grunall says, "Humility is the necessary veil to all other graces."

For Reflection

1. *For you personally, what is the scariest thing about giving consideration to setting your own agenda aside and why?*

2. *Of the five "secrets" noted in this chapter, which one do you find most useful to helping you step outside yourself to more accurately see your partner? And why did you select this one over the other four?*

3. *This chapter closes with an emphasis on humility. Do you agree that this is an essential bedrock to having an "agendaless presence"? Why or why not?*

Exercise Four
Checking Your Ego at the Door

Trading places begins when you first set aside your agenda before trying to diagnose, influence, or prescribe. Why? Because if you don't, you end up acting on assumptions that may be totally incorrect. And that is guaranteed to lead to trouble. So in this exercise you'll learn the easy way to check your ego at the door and temporarily set aside what's on your agenda so you can effectively start the process of trading places. Once you master this skill, you'll be amazed at how your spouse will want to do the same for you.

CHAPTER 5

I Feel with You
Turning on Your Emotional Radar

A finely tuned ear is at the heart of empathy.
Daniel Goleman

"Shhh."

"What's going on?" I whispered.

Les was sitting on the couch in our living room watching the classic movie *Gone with the Wind*—but the sound was turned off as he sat there transfixed. I quietly walked toward him to feel his forehead.

"I'm not sick," he grunted. "Sit down and watch this."

I was quiet for a moment and then asked, "You realize the volume is off, right?"

"I know, but watch their faces."

That's when I gazed around the living room to see if I was being set up for a hidden camera show.

"Are you alright?" I asked.

"Yes," he replied, "just watch this for a minute and tell me what you feel."

"What I *feel*? I can already tell you—I feel like you're going bonkers."

Les pressed the pause button and let me in on his strange behavior.

"I guess this does look weird," he confessed, "but I was talking to Jim at the university and he told me that he has all of his freshman acting students watch this movie with the sound off so that they can see the power of communicating emotions without words."

"Really?" I said with genuine intrigue. "Turn it back on and let me see."

For the next few minutes we sat in silence as Scarlett O'Hara did her best to make Ashley jealous by surrounding herself with boys at a barbecue.

About that time, John, our nine-year-old, walked into the living room to see his parents watching a movie in silence and asked: "Is the TV broken?"

Nope. Just another day in the home of two psychologists. The little exercise is actually quite powerful. It's a quick study in how much can be conveyed nonverbally. And it's a lesson every spouse who wants to master the second major step in trading places can learn: turning on your emotional radar.

Detecting Your Partner's Wavelength

You know radar as a system used to manage air traffic control, monitor weather patterns, and enforce the speed limit on our highways. You may not immediately see its relevance to trading places, but consider what's going on through radar: A transmitter emits radio waves, which are reflected by the target and detected by a receiver. That's all.

You can no doubt see where we're going with this. But what's important to realize, for our purposes, is that a radio signal, though very weak, can still be detected by radar. In fact, that's what radar does best. It picks up on signals that are being missed and amplifies them.

And that's exactly what emotional radar is all about. When you learn to pick up on emotional signals that your spouse is transmitting, when you tune into them, you are practicing the second step of trading places. It all comes down to detecting your partner's emotions.

Now, if you are thinking to yourself that you're no good at picking up on other people's emotions, rest easy. You're probably better at it than you think. But even if you aren't—and there are some people who find this to be more challenging than others—we're going to give you practical tools for drastically improving your capacity to detect the emotional signals your spouse is sending out.

> He who does not understand your silence will probably not understand your words.
>
> **Elbert Hubbard**

And keep in mind that if you're reading this together, your spouse will be learning to do the same thing for you.

Everyone Can Improve Their Emotional Radar

Ron was hired by an environmental institute that is dedicated to preserving an endangered species of bighorn sheep that live in the mountains just southwest of Palm Springs, California. Development of neighboring land was disturbing the sheep and interrupting their breeding activity, so the institute wanted to do something about it.

When Ron visited the institute, the director took him outside, pointed to the massive rocky hills that roll up behind the offices, and said softly, "There are a lot of them out today." Ron squinted up at the brown hills, trying to hide his amazement—not at the beauty of the bighorn sheep, but at his inability to see even one of them. Obviously accustomed to this reaction, the director tact-fully called his attention to a sheep just below a triangular rock, and another on the crest of a hill to the left, and then another and another. Ron soon began to see dozens.

The director's eyesight was no better than Ron's. But he had learned to see the sheep. He knew how their shape broke the subtle patterns of the hills. He could detect the slight difference between their color and that of the rock. What was virtually automatic to him was foreign to Ron, until he too learned to see the sheep.

In much the same way, the person who learns to decode their spouse's emotional radar signals sees cues and messages that the untrained eye repeatedly misses.[1] They scan the social scene with their partner for important details to guide their actions. They not only listen to the words being spoken, they observe their spouse's nonverbals. They pay attention to voice tone, facial expressions, and eye contact.[2] They are tuned in to unspoken feelings and are sensitive to signals that convey their partner's heart.

Researchers believe that about 90 percent of emotional com-munication is nonverbal. Harvard psychologist Robert Rosenthal developed an assessment of people's ability to read emotional cues called the Profile of Nonverbal Sensitivity (PONS).[3] He shows subjects a film of a young woman expressing feelings like anger, jealousy, love, and gratitude. Unbeknownst to the viewer, one or another nonverbal cue has been edited out. In some instances, the face is visible but not the body, or the woman's eyes are hidden, so the viewers have to judge the feeling by subtle cues. People with higher PONS scores, even if their IQs are quite average, tend to be more successful in marriages, enjoying a deeper connection and more happiness. What's more, everyone can learn to improve their PONS score. In other words, everyone—from the novice to the expert—can get better at detecting their partner's emotions. And everyone has a predisposition to do just that.

You Are Hardwired
for Emotional Radar

Scientists call them "mirror neurons." They discovered them as they were mapping areas of the brain with laser-thin electrodes — so thin they could be implanted into a single brain cell. And in 1992, by accident, they found that certain cells lit up during particular interpersonal exchanges. They lit up whenever a person would reflect back an action observed in someone else, mimicking that action or having the impulse to do so.[4] These mirror neurons offer a brain mechanism that explains the old lyric, "When you're smiling, the whole world smiles with you."

Technically, this recently discovered mirroring process is referred to as "social synchrony." And the point of it all is to underscore how we humans are hardwired with emotional radar. We are designed to pick up on subtle cues from each other, especially in marriage. For example, if a scientist were to monitor a particular and single mirror neuron in your brain as you were about to receive a shot from

> Our nervous systems are constructed to be captured by the nervous systems of others, so that we can experience others as if from within their skin.
>
> **Daniel Stern**

your doctor, that neuron would fire. No surprise. But if you were merely asked to imagine your spouse was about to receive that shot instead of you, that same mirror neuron would still fire.[5] Isn't that remarkable? It's called primal empathy. Deep in your brain you are hardwired to empathize with your spouse. You have an internal radar system that allows you to enter his or her world more easily than you might have thought.

What's more, you and your spouse are not only hardwired for empathy as individuals, the circuitry of your brains is built to bring you closer together when you do so. Giacomo Rizzolati, the Italian neuroscientist who discovered mirror neurons, explains that the triggering of parallel circuitry in two brains lets us instantly achieve a shared sense of what matters most in any given moment. In other words, when we trade places, we experience a shared immediacy or bonding at the deepest levels. Neuroscientists call that mutually reverberating state "empathic resonance."[6] It's that profound contentment that comes from a heretofore unknown brain-to-brain linkage that results in living in harmony.

Our goal in this chapter is to help you more readily turn on those mirror neurons in your brain, activate your emotional radar, and thus understand exactly what your partner is experiencing.

Why Doesn't Empathy Happen More Often?

Before we help you amp up your emotional radar, we want to answer a question you may be asking: If we are hardwired for empathy, why doesn't it happen more often?

In short, the answer is "lack of attention." You see, our brains may have the circuitry and inclination to trade places, but our empathic neurons won't fire if we don't give another person our attention. In other words, we've got to "tune into" our partner to activate our brain for empathy. You may have a radio in your home, but you'll never hear music from it until you tune into a station that's emitting a signal. And if you were to turn it on and hear nothing but static, you'd focus your attention on finding a station that would come in. Well, just as you might adjust the knob on your radio to fine-tune the reception of a radio signal, you've got to adjust your attention to focus on your partner. Otherwise empathy doesn't have a chance. Paying attention allows us to turn on our emotional radar.

To say it another way, your capacity for trading places is strongest when you are focused on your spouse. No big surprise, right? But think about what this means. This means being alert. Listening carefully. Staying watchful and observant.

Most of the time we can direct or inhibit our attention. In the example of getting a shot from your doctor, you are almost certain to give that attention. Pain, in fact, is one of the great primal attention grabbers. You can't help but to focus your attention on it. But seeing your wife at the sink doing dishes? Not so much. You're not compelled to focus on her experience at that moment. And sadly, some couples rarely dedicate their attention to their spouse. In the busyness and hum-drum of life, they suffer from what we call the "marriage trance." They fall into a self-absorbed state and eventually become the two proverbial ships passing in the night, never taking serious notice of each other's emotions—never giving each other attention. That's why empathy doesn't happen more often.

Of course, it doesn't have to be that way.

Activating Your Emotional Radar

You already know that words communicate only a little of what your spouse really thinks, feels, or means. In fact, sometimes words do not communicate much at all. Research shows that face-to-face communication regarding attitudes and feelings is 7 percent what people say, 38 percent how they say it, and 55 percent body language.[7]

People's emotions are rarely put into words; far more often they are expressed through other cues: tone of voice, gestures, facial expressions, and the like. A common rule of thumb used in communications research is that 90 percent or more of an emotional message is nonverbal.

The question is, how can you tune into these nonverbal messages? How can you read emotions that aren't being articulated? Once you tune into your partner with your attention, how do you activate your emotional radar?

It comes back around to the secret we revealed in the first chapter of this book. Do you remember? It's the secret most couples don't know: Empathy calls for loving your partner with both your head and heart concurrently. Most of us do one or the other pretty well; we either feel our partner's pain with our heart, or we try to solve their problem with our head. To do both is what empathy demands.

So with this in mind, let's take a look at what you can do on a very personal level to activate your emotional radar. First, you need to review your results from the online Trading Places Inventory (if you haven't taken it yet, you can do so at www.RealRelationships. com). Are you more of a Sympathizer, a Personalizer, or an Analyzer? Or do you have a strong combination of more than one of these? Whatever your situation, focus on the following portions of this chapter that have the most relevance to you.

What to Do If You Are a Sympathizer

As you know from the Trading Places Inventory, your sympathetic leanings outweigh your analytic inclinations. In other words, your heart takes precedence over your head. This means that the challenge for you in activating your emotional radar will be to gain a more objective perspective than you are used to when tuning into your spouse. You will need to step back from your own emotions that often drive you and press the pause button. You'll need to ask yourself if you are projecting your own emotions onto your partner before you accurately understand them.

Laura Hillenbrand, author of the acclaimed *Seabiscuit*, the 2001 nonfiction account of a great racehorse, has long suffered from chronic fatigue syndrome, a debilitating condition that left her exhausted and needing constant care for months at a time. While she was writing *Seabiscuit*, she received care from her devoted husband, Borden, who somehow found the energy to be her nurse even while struggling with his own work as a graduate student. He helped her eat and drink. He assisted her when she needed to walk and so on.

> *When we understand another's viewpoint, understand what he is trying to do, nine times out of ten he is trying to do right.*
>
> **Harry Truman**

In her bedroom one night, Hillenbrand recalls hearing a "soft, low sound." She looked down the stairway to see Borden "pacing the foyer and sobbing." She started to call out to him but stopped herself, realizing he wanted to be alone. The next morning, Borden was there to help her as usual, "cheerful and steady as ever."[8]

What caused Laura Hillenbrand to pause? Why didn't she call out to her sobbing husband to comfort him? It was her emotional radar. He didn't say a word. In fact, he had no idea she was even aware of him. But she was. And her emotional radar told her to back off and let him have some space.

That's a valuable lesson for every Sympathizer. Why? Because you are so inclined to let your feelings guide you. And if you see your spouse crying, for example, your emotional impulse is to rush in. But if you pause, just for a moment, and use your analytic abilities to consider your spouse — asking yourself *What would my partner want in this moment?* — you fine-tune your emotional radar and become more adept at this important second step toward trading places.

We realize this may rub you the wrong way. We realize that as a Sympathizer you often take on a great deal of personal responsibility for your spouse's well-being. You are more inclined than others, for example, to ruminate about upsetting exchanges you have with him or her. And because of this you pay an emotional price. Your emotional perspective causes you to be so focused on the ups and downs of your relationship (without the desired analytic balance), that you are susceptible to riding an emotional roller coaster in your marriage.[9]

> An understanding heart is everything and cannot be esteemed highly enough.
>
> Carl Gustav Jung

Not only that, but you are also susceptible to what researchers call "empathy distress" or "compassion fatigue." Because you feel so deeply what you perceive your partner's pain to be, for example, your own anxiety about it can become overpowering until you begin to meet needs that don't exist.

It's like the story of the two Cub Scouts whose younger brother had fallen into a lake. They rushed home to Mother with tears in their eyes. One of them sobbed, "We tried to give him CPR, but he kept getting up and walking away."

Or consider Rita, an only child, who grew up in a home where she felt cherished by a mom and dad who went out of their way to care for her. They were continually looking after Rita and each other. So when Rita married Vince, the middle child in a family with several siblings, she made the erroneous assumption so many people make in marriage, that "what's good for me is good for you." She cared for him the way she wanted to be cared for. She brought him snacks, for example, whether he was hungry or not. She saw this as an act of kindness. He saw it as a waste of food. She would set out a clean shirt for him to wear in the morning. She saw this as being thoughtful. He saw it as being smothered. It was all too much for Vince.

So much "caring" became downright irritating to him. Rita had no idea why he was so often annoyed. Rita thought she was helping when, in truth, she was only making matters worse. It's nothing personal. Vince simply feels smothered by too much caring. The point? Rita will never succeed in loving Vince until she first puts herself in his shoes—not only with her heart but with her head as well (the same is true, by the way, for Vince).

Without objectivity, without an analytical perspective, your emotions get the better of you, and before long, you'll burn out from your own anguish or exhaustion when faced with an inordinate amount of suffering.

So, once again, your goal as a Sympathizer is to lean into your analytical capacities by pressing your emotional pause button and checking out your partner's feelings before you make emotional assumptions. In other words, don't let your feelings cloud your objectivity.

What to Do If You Are a Personalizer

If the results of your Trading Places Inventory indicate that you are a Personalizer, you know that your task is to cultivate a more other-focused agenda. You've got to consciously step outside yourself and give greater attention to imagining what a specific moment in time would be like for your spouse. You need to do this with both your head and your heart. You need to *think* it through as well as *feel* it through.

There is an old Chinese tale about a woman whose only son died. In her grief, she went to a holy man and said, "What magical incantations do you have to bring my son back to life?" Instead of sending her away or reasoning with her, he said to her, "Fetch me a mustard seed from a home that has never known sorrow. We will use it to drive the sorrow out of your life."

The woman set off at once in search of that magical mustard seed. She came first to a splendid mansion, knocked at the door, and said, "I am looking for a home that has never known sorrow. Is this such a place? It is very important to me." They told her, "You've certainly come to the wrong place," and began to describe all the tragic things that had recently befallen them. The woman said to herself, "Who is better able to help these poor unfortunate people than I, who have had misfortune of my own?" She stayed to comfort them, then went on in her search for a home that had never known sorrow. But wherever she turned, in hovels and palaces, she found one report after another of sadness and misfortune.

Ultimately, the woman became so involved in ministering to other people's grief that she forgot about her quest for the magical mustard seed, never realizing it had, in fact, driven the sorrow out of her life.

This is the great lesson for every Personalizer: You will never move beyond the hurts of your life until you realize that trading places is your ticket out of them. Your self-focus, while understandable, is sabotaging the very thing you want most — to move forward and live a life of love and happiness.

Look beyond your own neediness to the needs of your spouse and watch how empathy can take root in your heart. We know that may sound pat or even glib, but it's true. We also know that as a Personalizer, you are probably carrying a fair bit of emotional pain in your life. So, as we mentioned in an earlier chapter, don't forget to turn to appendix B. It's filled with a practical plan for helping you move beyond your hurts and turn on your emotional radar.

What to Do If You Are
an Analyzer

Pillsbury. Cheerios. Green Giant. Betty Crocker. Chex. What do all these famous brands have in common? They are all owned by General Mills, one of the world's largest consumer products manufacturers. And from a sales perspective, one of the biggest brands in the company's history has been Hamburger Helper. But sales of this well-known brand have been in decline for nearly a decade. Or we should say they *had* been in decline, but no more. And General Mills has Melissa Studzinski to thank for that.

When Melissa joined the team in 2004, the CEO announced that the number one goal of the company was to grow Hamburger Helper. He put Melissa in charge, arming her with three huge binders full of data and statistics about the product. The binders contained hundreds of pages about sales and volume data, advertising-strategy briefs, market research, and so on. Melissa did her best to study the contents of these binders and wrap her head around the data. But the more she studied the facts, the more elusive was her strategy. She eventually called them her "death binders." Why? Because all of the analytic information was keeping her from understanding her customers—the people she was trying to serve.

> An ounce of emotion is equal to a ton of facts.
>
> John Junor

So Melissa put the data aside and tried something new. She made plans to send members of the Hamburger Helper team, staffers from marketing and advertising, for example, into the homes of Hamburger Helper customers. They found mothers who were willing to let strangers come into their homes and watch them as they cooked. The team visited about three dozen homes. And that's when their sales began to spike.

"I had read and I could recite all the data about our customers," Melissa says. "I knew their demographics by heart. But it was a very different experience to walk into a customer's home and experience a little bit of her life."[10]

It was the more emotional side of empathy that made the difference for Melissa and her eventual success. But did you catch that phrase she used—"experience a little bit of her life"? This is key for you as an Analyzer. As you know from the results of your Trading Places Inventory, your analytic leanings outweigh your sympathetic inclinations. In other words, your head takes precedence over your heart. This means that the challenge for you in activating your emotional radar will be to gain a more sympathetic perspective than you are used to when tuning into your spouse. For example, if you find yourself getting trigger happy to solve her problem before you've taken the time to fully understand it, you've got to press the pause button on your analytic acumen and allow some space for your emotions—as well as hers—to enter the picture.

> People don't ask for facts in making up their minds. They would rather have one good, soul-satisfying emotion than a dozen facts.
>
> **Robert Keith Leavitt**

After all, you are likely to remain rational and detached, as opposed to emotional and absorbed if you aren't intentional. That's okay. But when it comes to trading places with your partner, your analytic ways can only go so far. You need to experience a little bit of your spouse's life. That means allowing your heart, not just your head, to play a role.

How to Read Your Partner
Like a Book

"I'm no psychologist," a disgruntled husband recently told us. "How can I be expected to understand my wife's feelings—half the time I don't even think *she* knows what she's feeling!"

Of course, this sentiment goes both ways: "I never know what my husband is thinking, let alone what he's feeling," a wife might say. "He keeps his emotions so hidden, you'd have to be a detective to find out what he's feeling."

Truth is, you don't have to be Columbo to uncover your spouse's emotions. Whether you are a Sympathizer, a Personalizer, or an Analyzer, the emotions of every husband and wife are easier to detect than you might imagine. Even when people try to conceal their feelings, their true emotions are likely to show. Research proves it. So in concluding this chapter on the second important step to trading places—turning on your emotional radar—we wanted to leave you with this encouraging study.

A videotaped study of unhappy couples at the University of Oregon explored how emotions are emitted even when those emotions are disguised. The experimenters told the stressed couples that their task was to "fool the cameras" and pretend they were happily married. They asked the couples to make believe they had just been given a large sum of money and they had to decide together how to spend it.

Looking at the printed transcripts of the couples' conversations, you'd never know they weren't exceedingly

> There are moments in life, when the heart is so full of emotion that if by chance it be shaken, or into its depths like a pebble drops some careless word, it overflows, and its secret, spilt on the ground like water, can never be gathered together.
>
> **Henry Wadsworth Longfellow**

happy. In fact, most of them faked being happy quite well. The words show them to be loving, respectful, and conflict-free. But if you watch and listen to the video tapes of the couples' conversations, you get a very different impression. Their facial expressions, body language, and voice tones betray their performances at every turn.

Lines like, "Whatever you say, dear" and "It's up to you" are punctuated with sarcasm and contempt. "Their interactions are like sieves, leaking hostility everywhere," said one researcher. In fact, that's the verb psychologists use to describe the way we involuntarily show our emotions: Our feelings "leak" through.[11]

Imagine that! Even if a person is trying to conceal their real feelings, we often pick up on them. Now, think of what this says about how much easier it is to access your spouse's feelings when they are real! If nothing else, this should underscore for you just how available your partner's emotions are to you when you simply take a moment to attend to them — when you turn on your emotional radar.

And once you do that — once you set aside your own agenda (temporarily) and once you turn on your emotional radar — you have just one more essential step to guarantee the full benefits of trading places.

For Reflection

1. In general, how important is it to you to be able to better read your partner's emotions? By improving in this area, how do you believe it will improve your marriage? Be specific.

2. Are you more of a Sympathizer, a Personalizer, or an Analyzer? And with your interpersonal style in mind, what is one practical thing you will do to become better at trading places? And when will you do it?

3. The chapter closes with an encouraging word about your emotional radar — that it's easier to read your partner's emotions than you might think. Do you agree with this? Why or why not? And if not, do you think your negative expectation is interfering with your ability to read your partner? How so?

Exercise Five
Reading Your Partner Like a Book

Wouldn't it be wonderful to find a book in your home with the title *My Spouse's Feelings Right Now?* You could refer to it whenever you wanted to tune into his or her emotions and know exactly what's going on. Well, we can't give you that book, but in this particular exercise we will give you something that comes pretty close. We'll lead you to a deeper understanding of your spouse's emotions so that you can more quickly and easily identify them whenever you like.

CHAPTER 6

I Act to Help You
Demonstrating Your Care Quotient

Empathy alone matters little if we fail to act.
James D. Parker

Would it make any difference if you could go back in time and observe firsthand the kind of home your spouse came from? What if you could observe some of the most significant experiences he or she had as a child? Would this ability to personally relive portions of his or her life make a difference for you? Surely it would.

It did just that for former Minnesota Vikings football player Doug Kingsriter. He writes about a time when he and his wife Debbie got stranded at her parents' home for three days because of an ice storm. With plenty of time to kill, Doug ended up watching all of Debbie's home movies that her family had made over the years. He watched how her family celebrated her birthdays and how she worked to be Miss Teenage America. He saw how her parents interacted, the models of marriage they provided Debbie.

"I literally watched her grow up," Doug said. "By the third day, I realized the girl in the films was the same person I'd married ... it allowed me to really see Debbie for the first time."

Doug called this experience of entering her world a "moment of awakening" in his marriage. "From then on, I listened much more closely to Debbie ... I treated her with more respect."[1]

Empathy has a way of doing that. It changes you. It awakens you to a new way of acting. And acting is the third essential step to trading places. Once you set aside your own agenda (temporarily), and once you turn on your emotional radar, you are ready to take action. You are ready to demonstrate a new level of understanding toward your spouse.

Here's the sequence, once again, in short:

> I notice you,
> I feel with you, and so
> I act to help you.

It's in the "acting to help" where the payoff of trading places occurs. The first two steps are a mere means to get you and your partner to a new place where acts of kindness, consideration, and benevolence envelop your relationship.[2] As we often say in our Trading Places seminars, to feel *with* stirs us to act *for*.

The First Sign
of Full-Fledged Empathy

One day a student asked famed anthropologist Margaret Mead for the earliest sign of civilization in a given culture. He expected the answer to be a clay pot or perhaps a fishhook or grinding stone. Her answer was "a healed femur." Mead explained that no healed femurs are found where the law of the jungle, survival of the fittest, reigns. A healed femur shows that someone cared. Someone had to do that injured person's hunting and gathering until the leg healed. The evidence of compassion, said Mead, is the first sign of civilization.[3]

And it's also the first sign that a spouse is demonstrating full-fledged empathy. No act of true empathy has ever been displayed in the absence of care and concern. Without it, "empathy" becomes a cruel tool of manipu-

> After the verb "to love," "to help" is the most beautiful verb in the world.
>
> **Bertha von Suttner**

lation and self-centeredness. Even a sociopath is able to set aside his own agenda (temporarily) and get his victim to open up. He can even turn on his emotional radar to better understand what makes his victim tick. But that's where the process ends. He has no concern or care for the person. He's simply gathering personal information about the person to take advantage of them.

Genuine empathy, of course, uses the first two steps for an entirely different purpose — to demonstrate care and concern, to heal a broken femur, as it were.

That's why we dedicate this chapter to helping you put your empathy into action. After all, what good is it if your spouse knows what was going on for you and feels it deeply but doesn't do anything about it? And what good would it be for your spouse if you did the same? That's why care is inextricably connected to genuine empathy — it compels you to take action.

A Happy Marriage = A Positive Care Quotient

Tina thought for a moment, shrugged her shoulders, then confessed: "I guess I just stopped caring."

Like other spouses who have sat in our counseling office just before heading to a divorce attorney, Tina had crossed a line that is often lethal. Once a person moves to the point of not caring, the relationship is on life support and the prospect of survival is grave.

When you remove care from any relationship, it's over. There's nothing left to discuss. It's like removing blood from the body. Marriage, in any meaningful form, cannot survive without care.

> Love is, above all, the gift of oneself.
>
> **Jean Anouilh**

Care is so germane, so essential to marriage, that it often goes unnoticed. Ask people what matters most in marriage and care won't make the list. But when you put this quality on a list of traits and ask people to rate its importance to marriage, you'll see it quickly rise. Why? Because without care, marriage is impossible. Three little words—"I don't care"—are like a deadly bullet in the heart of marriage.

Frank Reed may understand the value of caring as well as anyone we know. From 1986 to 1990, he was held hostage in a Lebanon jail cell. He was blindfolded for months at a time, living in complete darkness. He was chained to a wall and kept in absolute silence. On one occasion, Reed was moved to another cell, and, although blindfolded, he could sense others in the room. Only weeks later did he learn he was chained next to fellow American hostages Terry Anderson and Tom Sutherland.

In his years as a prisoner, Reed was humiliated, beaten, made ill, and tormented. But it was none of these horrific conditions that pained Reed the most as a hostage. It was the intolerable lack of concern by his captors. It was not knowing if anyone cared. In an interview with *Time*, Reed said, "Nothing I did mattered to anyone. I began to realize how withering it is to exist with not a single expression of caring around me ... I learned one overriding fact: caring is a powerful force. If no one cares, you are truly alone."[4]

The Essence of
Your Care Quotient

It seems funny that we toss this vital force around so, well, carelessly. "Take care," we say to the grocery clerk who rings up our items. "Take care," we say at the end of a phone conversation with a near stranger. But when was the last time you took time to consider what "taking care" really means?

The word "care" comes from the Germanic *kar*, which originally meant "sad." It alludes to the idea that a caring person feels sad when you feel sad. In other words, care is a kind of compassion that allows someone to enter your world and feel your pain. Care is inextricably linked to trading places. It says that whatever happens to you happens to me, when sadness hits you, it hits me too. Of course, care also says that when something terrific happens to you, I rejoice myself. Your life makes a genuine difference to my own life. That's the essence of your care quotient.

When we truly care for our spouse — at a deep and meaningful level — we involve both our heart and our head. We think our spouse's thoughts and feel our spouse's emotions. When we care for our partner, we listen and watch for ways to be helpful. We take notice and attend to her world as if it were our own. It's what Aristotle was getting at when he referred to the idea of "a single soul dwelling in two bodies."

You don't have to be a hostage to appreciate the powerful force of care. All of us practice caring instinctively on occasion.[5] Like handling a costly crystal vase, we're careful with things we value. And if your spouse has had to cope with a serious accident or life-threatening illness, you don't need a book to show

> You're blessed when you care. At the moment of being "care-full," you find yourselves cared for.
>
> Matthew 5:7 (MSG)

you how to care. The needle of your care quotient jumps to its greatest possible capacity. But the normal hum-drum of life, when we tend to take each other for granted, doesn't do much to jump-start our care quotient — unless we're trading places.

How to Improve Your Care Quotient

In the first chapter of this book we said that whenever a couple neglects to trade places, when they sidestep empathy, they become clueless. Quite literally, they become ignorant about each other. However, we also said that these couples who lack empathy don't necessarily lack love. That is, they still want a better way of living and loving together. They're simply baffled by their spouse's feelings, thoughts, and behaviors. They're clueless.

> Love is not a single act, but a climate in which we live, a lifetime venture in which we are always learning, discovering, growing.
>
> **Ardis Whitman**

But with a little effort, even the most clueless couples on the planet can become unimaginably smarter when they practice the three essential steps to trading places — especially when they get to this third step. Why? Because your "care quotient," unlike your IQ, can improve dramatically at will. You can instantly increase your care quotient by *doing* what your empathic understanding guides you to.

Now we could give you a long list of potential caring behaviors that result from trading places. We could tell you to take time for tender touches or to put your spouse's needs before your own. But that would be so pedantic. Besides, we can't tell you exactly what actions are going to be the actions your spouse would desire. Only your empathic efforts will reveal that. So instead of prescribing caring behaviors for you to emulate, we are going to provide you with a bit of inspiration followed by a challenge. The inspiration will come in the form of a couple of stories. The challenge will come from the heart.

We start with the first story told by Jennifer Rothschild, author of *Lessons I Learned in the Dark*. At the young age of fifteen, Susan was diagnosed with a rare, degenerative eye disease that would eventually steal her sight. Rothschild tells this story:

A Salute and a Kiss

It was a very crowded bus, and all the passengers looked sympathetically as Susan made her way down the aisle. She fumbled with her cane, and as she nestled herself into her seat, the onlookers just watched with questions and concern. You see, it had been a year since Susan lost her sight.

When she first became blind, she fell into a deep pit of depression. Her world had crumbled, her sadness overtook her. Not only was her heart crushed, but so was the heart of her husband, Mark. He so loved his wife and wanted to help her, and so he did. Inch by inch, he helped to pull her out of that pit of depression, helped give her skills and confidence, and helped her to regain her sense of self. And that husband, so in love with his wife, did all that he could to help her in her new state of darkness.

Well, after many months of Susan's blindness, she began to feel more confident because of Mark's help, and she felt like she could perhaps return to her job again. And Mark promised that he would help her, of course, with that also. So every day, Mark would drive his wife to work, walk her into the office, make sure she was settled, and then leave and go to his base that was across town, because Mark was

> Words can sometimes, in moments of grace, attain the quality of deeds.
>
> **Eli Wiesel**

121

a military officer. Then, he would come back and get her from work. This went on for several weeks. And with every day, though Mark so wanted to help his wife, the burden was becoming heavier because it was becoming logistically impossible for him to make it to his base on time.

He dreaded having to announce to Susan that he wasn't going to be able to drive her to work. But in the end, he had to. "I can't ride the bus to work," she replied. "I'm blind. How am I going to know how many stairs there are? How am I going to know what path to take? I feel like you are abandoning me."

Mark's heart was crushed. He promised her, like he had done from the very beginning, he would do whatever it took to help her until she felt confident and independent on the bus. He helped her with the routes. He helped her learn the stairs and learn the paths. And so, finally, after several weeks of doing this, Susan was confident. He went to his base; she went to her work.

> The supreme happiness in life is the conviction that we are loved — for ourselves, or rather, in spite of ourselves.
>
> Victor Hugo

Monday morning, she got on the bus. She went to work, she came home; it was flawless. Then Friday morning arrived. Susan made her way onto the bus, and as she went to pay her fare, the bus driver said, "Ma'am you sure are lucky." Susan said, "Are you talking to me?" The bus driver said, "Yeah. It must feel good to be cared for as you are." Susan replied, "I don't know what you mean, sir."

The bus driver said: "Well, you know, every morning when I drop you off at your stop, as soon as those doors open, I can see that man standing over there at the corner. And he watches you. As soon as you step off the bus, his eyes are on you. I think he's some kind of military officer because of his uniform. And his eyes follow you as you walk across that parking lot. And his eyes don't leave you as you're trying to walk up those stairs. And when your hand touches that door knob, his eyes are on you. Until you open that door and go inside, that man doesn't take his eyes off you. And once that door closes, he stands straight and tall, like a sentinel, and he salutes you, and then he blows you a kiss."

Susan burst into tears. She had no idea that her husband had been watching her.[6]

How would you rate this husband's care quotient? And how many miles do you think he walked in Susan's shoes? We'll say it again: Care is inextricably linked to trading places. The more you empathize, the more you care.

Now for the second story, a legend, really. It's been passed down through Jewish traditions.

> In some sense the most benevolent, generous person in the world seeks his own happiness in doing good to others, because he places his happiness in their good. His mind is so enlarged as to take them, as it were, into himself.
>
> **Jonathan Edwards**

A Place of Love

The story is of two brothers who shared a field and a mill, each night dividing the grain they had ground together during the day. One brother lived alone; the other was married with a large family.

One day the single brother thought to himself, *It isn't fair that we divide the grain evenly. I have only myself to care for, but my brother has children to feed.* So each night he secretly took some of his grain to his brother's storehouse.

But the married brother considered his brother's situation, and said to himself, *It isn't right that we divide the grain evenly, because I have children to provide for me in my old age, but my brother has no one. What will he do when he's old?* So every night he secretly took some of his grain and put it in his brother's storehouse. As a result, both of the brothers found their supply of grain mysteriously replenished each morning.

> We make a living by what we get. We make a life by what we give.
>
> **Winston Churchill**

Then one night they met each other halfway between their two houses. They suddenly realized what the other was doing, and they embraced each other in love. The legend is that God witnessed their meeting and proclaimed, "This is a holy place — a place of love — and here it is that my temple shall be built."[7]

Apocryphal or not, this story illustrates the point that caring action flows from empathic understanding. And when trading places is mutual, as it was for these brothers, life doesn't get much sweeter.

Now for the challenge.

The Care Quotient Challenge

Whenever we teach counseling students at our university, we always use a simple metaphor to make the distinction between sympathy and empathy. It's an important distinction because professional counselors could never survive on mere sympathy. If they don't get a lock on empathy while working with their clients, their careers will be short-lived.

We tell our students that sympathy is standing on the shore and throwing a life ring out to a person who is struggling in the water. Every decent human being would do this. It flows with our adrenaline.

Empathy is much riskier. Empathy is diving into the water and thrashing around in the cold waves with that person to bring them to safety. Not everyone does that. In fact, it's so rare that we call the people who do "heroes." We put their picture in the paper and sometimes even have a parade.

Well, it can be just as heroic when we do this in our own marriage. Why? Because empathy *is* risky. It will change you. Once you immerse yourself in your partner's predicament or situation (with your head and heart), you won't look at him or her the same way. You'll have a new perspective that makes you more patient, more grace-giving, and more caring.

> What a grand thing, to be loved! What a grander thing still, to love!
>
> **Victor Hugo**

So this is our challenge to you as we conclude this chapter: Take the risk. We challenge you to take the risk of stepping in your partner's shoes by: (1) setting aside your own agenda (temporarily); (2) turning on your emotional radar; and (3) demonstrating your concern and care.

Empathy is not for cowards. It's risky business. But the risk is always worth it.

For Reflection

1. Do you agree that trading places means little if it doesn't change your behavior and cause you to act with care and kindness? When was the last time your empathy compelled you to do something especially caring for your partner? What was it?

2. What is one specific thing you can do in the next forty-eight hours for your spouse that would be sure to increase your personal Care Quotient? What, if anything, is likely to keep you from doing it?

3. How do you feel about the "Care Quotient Challenge"? Are you up to it? Why or why not? On what issue are you most reluctant to put yourself in your partner's shoes? In specific terms, how do you fear it might change you?

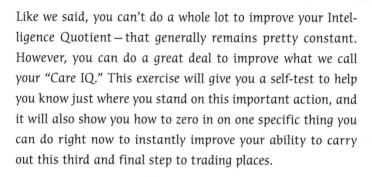

Exercise Six
Improving Your Care IQ

Like we said, you can't do a whole lot to improve your Intelligence Quotient—that generally remains pretty constant. However, you can do a great deal to improve what we call your "Care IQ." This exercise will give you a self-test to help you know just where you stand on this important action, and it will also show you how to zero in on one specific thing you can do right now to instantly improve your ability to carry out this third and final step to trading places.

PART THREE

HOW TO TRADE PLACES MORE QUICKLY

We've often fantasized about being able to see "signal bars" over each other's heads — like those in the cell phone commercials showing the bars going up and down to reflect varying cell phone reception. But instead of cell phone reception, these bars would show how much our partner understands what we are saying, feeling, or thinking. In other words, they would show us how well we are doing at trading places.

Wouldn't that make marriage easier? Imagine how much more quickly we could learn to trade places if we knew whether or not our message was getting through clearly.

Well, in a very real sense, the final chapter of this book will do just that. Of course, we can't provide you with tangible "signal bars," but we can point you to a specific means for ensuring a much stronger signal strength in your mutual efforts to step into each other's shoes.

This concluding part of the book will show you how to help your spouse see with your eyes and hear with your ears. In other words, this final chapter will give you practical ways of getting your spouse into your shoes. And as you

> When two people learn to *really* understand how the other feels at a deep and authentic level they have taken a quantum leap to a brilliant and unshakeable marriage.
>
> Neil Clark Warren

both take advantage of these strategies, you'll soon see mutual empathy take root in your marriage.

With these guidelines on "how to trade places more quickly," you won't have to struggle with a weak empathic signal. You'll know you're getting the best reception possible.

CHAPTER 7

Help Your Spouse
See Your Side

If a thing is worth doing,
it is worth doing badly.

G. K. Chesterton

Michelangelo called them his "Captives." You'll find all four of them standing in a great hall at a renowned museum in Florence, Italy. The famed sculptor had intended for each of them to be used on the tomb of Pope Julius. But midway through the project, he decided not to use them and ceased his work. Today anyone traveling to Florence can see the results—a hand protrudes here, a torso of a man there, a leg, part of a head. None of them are finished.

If you stand in this great hall, looking at these fragmentary figures, you will sense the turmoil, the struggle embodied in these stones. It's as though the figures are trying to break free from their blocks of marble to become what they were intended to be.

Have you ever felt like one of those "Captives"? Have you ever felt like a part of you was imprisoned or undiscovered? Maybe you've felt that your spouse isn't seeing an important part of you, that his or her empathy for you is only partial. Well, that's probably true. Like we said early on in this book, empathy often takes work.

> That is what marriage really means: helping one another to reach the full status of being persons, responsible and autonomous beings who do not run away from life.
>
> **Paul Tournier**

It often feels unfinished. That's why we dedicate this final chapter to helping you help your spouse to see the whole you. After all, you can do a great deal to make trading places easier for each other.

Did you know that you can "sculpt" your spouse? In scientific studies of marriage, it's literally called the Michelangelo Phenomenon. In subtle ways, you are reinforcing patterns in each other via countless little interactions. That sculpting can make it easier or tougher for your partner to see your point of view. We're here to show you how to make it easier. Much easier.

What follows are a half dozen tips that have proven helpful to many people who are trying to get their spouse to walk in their shoes. These are practical tips. You can put them to work for you starting today. We can't guarantee that every one of them will work for you, of course, but we can promise you that if you will give each of them a serious try, you'll discover a couple tips that will become especially helpful to you. We begin with an easy and painless way to help your spouse enter your world on a daily basis.

Share Your "Highs" and "Lows"

Here's a typical scenario in thousands of homes on a weekday evening when husband and wife are reunited after workdays:

"How was your day?" the wife asks as they greet each other at the front door.

"Fine," he replies as he picks up the paper along with the mail.

"Any news?" she asks while walking into the kitchen.

"Not really," he says while thumbing through envelopes of mostly bills and junk mail. "I landed the Perkins account so the boss was happy about that. How about you?"

"Oh, I talked with Sarah about next weekend and they're still not sure whether they can make it," she shouts from the kitchen.

"Hmm," he mutters as he plops into a chair, opens the paper, and kicks off his shoes.

And that concludes their interaction about their day. Sure, they'll pick up on a few more loose ends over dinner and maybe a few more if they happen to go to bed at the same time that evening. But that's about it.

Is it bad? Not really. Could it be better? You bet. Imagine the difference if they would take just five minutes to sit down face to face and review their day—not just *what* happened but how they *felt* about what

> You can't help someone get up a hill without getting closer to the top yourself.
>
> Norman Schwarzkopf

happened. Would their spirits be closer? Of course. And would they be more inclined to trade places throughout the remainder of their evening. Without a doubt! It would set the tone for more empathy and understanding for whatever else was to unfold that evening. Why? Because that five minutes becomes the portal for meaningful connection. When we know about a person's day, especially how they felt about it, we prime ourselves for trading places.

So here's our tip. If you want your partner to see the world from your point of view, take him or her through the highs and lows of your day. It doesn't take long. In fact, we've boiled it down to the mere minimum when we don't have the luxury of excess time. We simply ask each other, "What was your high and low since I've seen you last?" And with that we each tell the other about the best thing that happened while at work, and the worst.

So, the husband might say, "My high was when I finally landed the Perkins account—what a relief; and my low was when Jim critiqued my comments at the board meeting." This will inevitably lead to a few questions from his wife. And then it will be her turn. "My high was when Jacob's teacher told me that he's finally starting to focus in the classroom and really do well; and my low was when Sarah put off the decision about next weekend—it makes me feel like they don't want to be with us." Again, this will lead to a few questions for clarification and so on. That's it. The whole thing takes less than five minutes.

It's amazing how this little question opens up a window for viewing the emotional experience of our partner's day—and how it allows your partner to peer into yours. Try it right now with your spouse. Make it a daily habit. You'll soon see how sharing your "highs" and "lows" can help your spouse empathize with you.

Set Out the Right Pair of Shoes

Matt Emmons had the gold medal in sight. He was one shot away from claiming victory in the 2004 Olympic 50-meter three-position rifle event. He didn't even need a bull's-eye to win. His final shot merely needed to be on target. Anywhere on the target! It was a near guarantee that he'd win.

But something went terribly wrong. Emmons fired at the wrong target. Standing in lane two, he fired at the target in lane three. Normally, the shot he made would have received a score of 8.1, more than enough for a gold medal. But in what was described as "an extremely rare mistake in elite competition," Emmons missed his target altogether. His score for a good shot at the wrong target? Zero. Instead of a medal, Emmons ended up in eighth place.[1]

It doesn't matter how accurate you are if you are aiming at the wrong goal. We can almost sense you rolling your eyes at that last sentence. *That's obvious*, you might say. But we can tell you that in the countless couples we've counseled, we've seen far too many partners frustrated because they do precious little to make sure their spouse is aiming at the right target.

Here's the point. You've got to do whatever you can to help your partner target your experience. Too many times in marriage we play the guessing game — wanting our partner to know instinctively where to target their empathy. We come to believe that if my spouse loved me he would *know* how I feel without me telling him.

> The soul never thinks without a picture.
>
> **Aristotle**

But you *do* have to tell your spouse what you need and how you feel. We'll say it straight: Your partner can't read your mind. He may be an all-star at empathy, but that doesn't mean he's a mind reader. He still needs you to point him to the right target.

Allow us to put it another way: If you want your spouse to walk in your shoes, you've got to show him or her what shoes to step into. Don't leave your spouse guessing about what you're feeling.

Highlight Your Most Important Emotional Needs

We want to show you how voicing your needs can pave the way for your partner to walk in your shoes. The idea is to help your spouse get to the core of what makes you tick. You see, everyone has some relatively predictable psychological needs — needs that routinely rear their heads — and if you can highlight the big needs that are

> *Love takes off masks that we fear we cannot live without and know we cannot live within.*
>
> **James Baldwin**

specific to you, your partner will have a kind of shortcut to trading places with you.

For example, I (Les) have a fundamental emotional need to use my time wisely. I detest wasting time. I don't like to stand in long lines or be stuck in traffic or sit through a committee meeting going nowhere. I like to be efficient. This is a predictable trait for me. Now, you don't have to be a detective to figure this out. Leslie knows this about me. If she were asked to describe me to a stranger, she wouldn't need to be prompted to bring up this trait.

So why would I need to highlight this emotional trait for her? Because, like everyone else on the planet, Leslie has her own needs. And our own needs keep us from seeing our partner's. For example, one of Leslie's important emotional needs is to have approval. And if she isn't sensing my approval, her unmet need keeps her from remembering that time is a strong need for me. That's why I can help her trade places by saying things like, "My urgency needle is entering the red zone." Or "Don't forget that I'm not likely to put this task off." Statements like this keep my emotional needs in front of her.

Now, you can't expect your spouse to drop all of his or her needs just because you're highlighting your own. But you can expect your partner's potential for empathy to increase dramatically when you do this.

Of course, this tip is predicated on being able to articulate your top two or three emotional needs. The following list of common emotional needs may help you pinpoint yours.

Review this list and force yourself to eliminate all the secondary needs until you've narrowed it down to just your top two:

- ☐ Admiration
- ☐ Affection
- ☐ Approval
- ☐ Commitment
- ☐ Companionship
- ☐ Conversation
- ☐ Domestic Support
- ☐ Financial Security
- ☐ Forgiveness

- ☐ Honesty
- ☐ Humor
- ☐ Intimacy
- ☐ Loyalty
- ☐ Openness
- ☐ Respect
- ☐ Sexual Fulfillment
- ☐ Time
- ☐ Unity

Of course, this list is not exhaustive. You may think of an important emotional need that is not listed here. That's fine. This is simply a catalyst to help you identify your needs so that you can highlight them for your partner.

Once you've identified your top two needs, do your best to gently put them in front of your spouse when you think it would be helpful. Generally speaking, these are during times when one or both of you is feeling tired, hungry, or frustrated. Whenever your conversation is falling apart, you can say something like, "I know one of my biggest needs is admiration and I'm sure that's why I'm feeling especially unappreciated right now." Do you see what this does? It doesn't point fingers or sling guilt. It simply highlights your awareness of one of your big needs, and that will help your spouse enter your emotional world.

> Beyond the pairs of opposites of which the world consists, new insights begin.
>
> **Hermann Hesse**

Get Specific
with Your Gripes

Here's a simple do-it-yourself exercise that will underscore this practical tip.[2] Try it right now. Grab a pencil and a piece of paper. You'll also need a way to time yourself (a watch with a second hand). If you want to see how this works, don't read any further until you have your pen or pencil, your paper, and your timer. Ready?

Step One Instructions: Write down as many things that are white in color as you can think of. Start now and stop in fifteen seconds.

Once you've done this, proceed to the next step.

Step Two Instructions: Write down as many white things in your refrigerator as you can think of. Start now and stop in fifteen seconds.

How do your two lists compare?

Most people, remarkably, can list about as many white things from the small space of their refrigerator as they can when considering the entire universe. Stunning, isn't it? Not only that, but when we confine our consideration of white things to the defined space of our refrigerator, the exercise is actually easier.

Why is this so? Because concreteness helps our brain to focus more quickly and easily. That's why if you want your spouse to trade places with you on issues that are bugging you—not picking up clothes, running late, leaving lights on, spending money—you've got to make your gripes concrete.

If you want your spouse to see your point of view on an issue like being on time, don't say, "You always make us late." Instead, say something like, "When we're scheduled to teach the Sunday school class at our church and you're still getting dressed and doing your hair when it's 9:15, I start to feel really pressured and I can't focus on the lesson because I'm worried about what we'll say when we show up late. Do you know what I mean?"

This kind of specificity makes empathy far more likely. If you say, "You always make us late," that simply puts her on the defensive. But with a concrete description she can't help but to see it from your side. Not that this guarantees a complete turnaround, but it does make trading places possible.

Provide a Bit of Context

A little-known secret to interpersonal success is summed up this way: Context engenders caring. In other words, if a person understands the context for another person's experience, they are far more likely to care about that person. If you are upset, for example, and you want your spouse to understand and empathize with your emotions, you've got to let him in on the backstory. You've got to help him see what brought you to a place of feeling upset.

Consider this scenario: A husband and wife are in their bedroom getting dressed for a night on the town. The wife is telling her husband about a difficult interaction she had with a friend earlier that day. They are both sitting on the edge of their bed when he gets up and goes into his closet for a moment. That's when she stops talking and sends out a million nonverbal signals that she's upset. So her husband asks ...

"What's wrong?"

"You should know."

"Well, I don't so could you explain it to me? I thought we were having a conversation."

"If you don't know by now you'll never understand."

You know the experience, don't you? This quick exchange casts a cloud over the rest of their evening as each of them coils into their own corners of feeling misunderstood. It will only resolve when one of them conjures up an apology.

Now, compare that exchange to this one that begins with the same question from the husband:

"What's wrong?"

"You walked out on me while I was telling you about my meeting with Jennifer."

"I stepped into my closet for just a second to get my shoes — but I was still listening to you."

"I know, but when I was growing up, my dad used to walk out in the middle of conversations that he didn't want to hear, and every time you do that to me I feel like you're not interested and it hurts my feelings."

Do you think this husband is going to be better equipped to trade places? Of course. Why? Because his wife gave him the context for her feelings.

Context always makes empathy easier.

Give Your Spouse the Whole Picture

Sometimes your spouse needs more than a bit of context. He or she needs the whole picture.

Did you hear the Texas tall tale about the teacher who was helping one of her kindergarten students put on his cowboy boots? He asked for help, and she could see why. Even with her pulling and him pushing, the little boots still didn't want to go on. By the time they got the second boot on, she had worked up a sweat. She almost cried when the little boy said, "Teacher, they're on the wrong feet." She looked, and sure enough, they were.

It wasn't any easier pulling the boots off than it was putting them on. She managed to keep her cool as together they worked to get the boots back on, this time on the right feet. He then announced, "These aren't my boots."

She bit her tongue rather than get right in his face and scream, "Why didn't you say so?"

Once again, she struggled to help him pull the ill-fitting boots off his little feet. No sooner had they gotten the boots off when he said, "They're my brother's boots. My mom made me wear 'em."

Now she didn't know if she should laugh or cry, but she mustered up what grace and courage she had left to wrestle the boots on his feet again.

> The odds of hitting your target go up dramatically when you aim at it.
>
> **Mal Pancoast**

Helping him into his coat, she asked, "Now, where are your mittens?"

He said, "I stuffed 'em in the toes of my boots."

You may smile at how this little Texan dispensed portions of information that were only helpful if they'd been shared up front, but we do the same thing in conversations with our spouse and then wonder why they don't understand what we want.

"I'm going to need the car on Thursday evening."

"I was going to run some errands but that's okay. What's going on?"

"I've got to meet Ken for some stuff."

"What stuff?"

"He wants to connect on a work thing."

"Where are you meeting and maybe I can drop you off and then still have the car."

"No, I'll need the car the whole time."

"Why?"

"Because we're going to Tim's house right after we meet at Starbucks."

"Oh. What's happening at Tim's house?"

"He wants to show us this recording studio he built in his basement."

"Okay, maybe Ken could give you a lift."

"No, Tim is also going to install some speakers in the car."

"What?!"

"Yea, I got these cool speakers at a great price."

"Were you going to tell me about this?"

"What do you mean, I'm telling you right now."

"Only after I pieced your plans together. Why didn't you just tell me what you were doing right at the beginning?"

"Because I thought you'd be upset about me spending money on new speakers—and you are!"

This inane conversation could go on and on. It happens anytime a spouse, like this husband, is trying to achieve a goal without painting the full picture. And it's sure to sap your spouse of any capacity to trade places. Here's the alternative:

> To be alive is to be vulnerable.
>
> Madeleine L'Engle

"How would you feel about some new stereo speakers in our car?"

"Do we need them?"

"I don't know, but Tim is letting me have his old speakers at a bargain and he'll install them himself on Thursday night."

From there the conversation has a fighting chance of being rational, and this husband is far more likely to get his wife to trade places—all because she has the full picture.

A Quick Recap

We believe the content of this chapter is crucial to trading places. In our own marriage, in fact, we keep a list of these half dozen tips handy (posted on a mirror or on a desk). The list reminds us of exactly what to do to help us see the other person's perspective. Here it is:

* ⁎ Share your "highs" and "lows" — it will help your spouse experience your day.

* ⁎ Set out the right pair of shoes — it will keep your spouse from missing the mark.

* ⁎ Highlight your most important emotional needs — it will remind your spouse of your hardwiring.

* ⁎ Get specific with your gripes — it will increase your spouse's likelihood of doing something about complaints.

* ⁎ Provide a bit of context — it will tune your spouse into the meaning behind your emotions.

* ⁎ Give your spouse the whole picture — it will keep your spouse from having to play emotional games.

Each of these little tips, when practiced, will increase the odds of understanding each other. They will make trading places much more likely and ensure that your needs are getting met.

Before we end this chapter, we want to make one more important note on helping your spouse when it comes to trading places. It's a simple reminder to keep at it.

Keep Trying —
Even if You're Doing Badly

When it comes to trading places, we could not agree more with English writer G. K. Chesterton. Remember the quote at the opening of this chapter: "If a thing is worth doing, it is worth doing badly." After all, none of us will ever perfect the fine art of empathy. And that includes not only you, but your spouse.

Our friend Gary Thomas, author of *Sacred Marriage*, is an exceptionally bright thinker. We love the way he illustrates the reality of humanness in marriage. "If you were to divorce your spouse," he writes, "interview 200 'replacement' candidates, put them through a battery of psychological tests, have follow-up interviews conducted by your closest friends, spend three years dating the most compatible ones, and then another 40 days praying and fasting about which one to choose, you'd *still* end up with a spouse who disappoints you."[3]

> He who wrestles with us strengthens our nerves and sharpens our skill. Our antagonist is our helper.
>
> **Edmund Burke**

The point is, we are all human. Nobody's perfect. Sometimes our spouse will trade places beautifully. Sometimes our spouse will fail miserably. Each of you can only do so much to help the other see your point of view. You won't always succeed. But you can keep trying. So keep trying even if you're doing badly.

For Reflection

1. *What ways have you found on your own for getting your spouse to see the world from your point of view? What has worked for you in the past?*

2. *Of the six tips for getting your spouse to trade places with you, which one are you most excited about and why? When will you put it into practice?*

3. *The chapter closes with a reminder to keep trying when you feel like it's not going well. Why do you think this is important? At what time will this be especially important for you to remember?*

Exercise Eight
Getting Your Partner to See through Your Eyes

In this final exercise we will help you apply the content of this chapter at a personal level. We will make sure you are doing your very best to get your partner to see through your eyes. So get ready to roll up your sleeves and put the information in this chapter to work for you.

Why Every Couple Has a Chance at Trading Places

They know enough who know how to learn.

Henry Brooks Adams

Whenever we speak to couples on mutual empathy at one of our marriage seminars, someone will invariably come up to us during a break and ask, "Aren't some people incapable of empathy?"

Our answer is straightforward: only narcissists and deviants with no conscience.[1] Everyone else can use their head and heart to put themselves in their partner's shoes. It's been proven. Neuroscientists know we have something in our nature, right from the beginning, that provides the makings for human empathy. The capacity to see the world from another's perspective is in our DNA.[2]

For example, consider a content and comfortable newborn baby who hears another baby crying. The content baby also begins to wail. Research finds that it's not just the loud noise, but the sound of a fellow human in distress that triggers the baby's crying.[3]

Empathy is hardwired into us. There's no reason the two of you can't practice this skill and enjoy its rewards. But in this conclusion to our book, we want to warn you of the fact that some well-intentioned couples will never reap the benefits of trading places. For a variety of reasons, they will mute their natural capacity for mutual empathy and wonder why it's not working. That's why we feel compelled, in this conclusion, to warn you against these potential hazards:

- A lack of knowledge
- A lack of motivation
- A lack of prioritizing
- An unwillingness to change

These are the most common reasons even well-intentioned couples miss out on the promise of mutual empathy. In an effort to guard you from these hazards, let's take a closer look at each.

Some Never Trade Places Because They Don't Know How

My friend and mentor, John Maxwell, is a renowned expert on leadership. I (Les) had dinner with John in St. Louis not long ago and mentioned that Leslie and I were writing this book. John became animated. "That's so needed," he exclaimed. "I can't tell you how many people, even in prestigious places of leadership, simply don't know how to put themselves in another person's shoes."

Then, in John's predictably charismatic style, he told me a memorable story to underscore his point: A man in a hot air balloon realized he was lost. He reduced altitude and spotted a woman below. He descended a bit

> Willingness is essential in any initiation or in making a dream come true. "I can't" often means "I won't." You can change "I won't" to "I will" with willpower.
>
> **Marcia Wieder**

more and shouted, "Excuse me, can you help me? I promised a friend I would meet him an hour ago, but I don't know where I am." The woman below replied, "You're in a hot air balloon hovering approximately 30 feet above the ground. You're between 43 and 44 degrees north altitude and between 38 and 39 degrees west longitude."

"You must be an engineer," said the balloonist.

"Indeed, I am. How did you know?" the woman asked.

The balloonist answered: "Everything you told me is technically correct, but I've no idea what to make of your information, and the fact is, I'm still lost. Frankly, you've not been much help at all. If anything, you've delayed my trip."

The woman below responded, "You must be in management."

"Indeed, I am," replied the balloonist, "but how did you know?"

The woman answered: "Well, you don't know where you are or where you're going. You have risen to where you are due to a large quantity of hot air. You made a promise, which you've no idea how to keep, and you expect people beneath you to solve your problems. The fact is, you are in exactly the same position you were in before we met, but now, somehow, you've managed to make it my fault."

How many times in your marriage have you had a conflict because you see the situation one way and your spouse sees it another? It happens to us all. Inevitably, we bump heads because we don't share the same perspective. And if we don't know the ins and outs of mutual empathy, that's just where we'll remain — in conflict.

> We do not know the inmost depths of the human heart; it is revealed only to love. But those who condemn have generally little love, and therefore the mystery of the heart which they judge is closed to them.
>
> **Nicolas Berdyaev**

Of course, now that you have studied this book, you can't hang any excuses for a lack of empathy in your marriages on this reason. You now know how to trade places. You know how to put yourself in your partner's shoes and you know how to make it easier for your partner to do the same. So let's look at the next most common reason some don't practice empathy.

Some Never Trade Places Because They Don't Try

Ever imagined what it would be like to ride along a beam of light? No? Well, Albert Einstein did. In fact, it was his imagination and his penetrating "what if" questions about the universe that led Einstein to revolutionize our understanding of space and time. His imprint on science, needless to say, is legendary.

But what you may not know about Einstein is what James Gates Jr., an African American and a leading physicist, discovered. Einstein showed tremendous empathy for African Americans in his day and Gates saw a fascinating correlation between Einstein's capacity for scientific creativity and how his genius for imagination allowed him to "put himself in African-American shoes, just as he rode that beam of light."[4] In other words, Gates viewed Einstein's ability to ask "what if" as a propellant to empathy.

But Einstein's empathic genius fell short in his personal life. As biographer Tom Levenson says, it was hard to be Einstein's wife. Levenson, like many biographers, wrestled with the complexity of Einstein's humanity. As with other "great" human beings, Levenson suggests, one is tempted to idealize Einstein's genius and make him a saint. But Albert Einstein was no saint at home. He married Mileva in 1903 and soon delivered to her a long list of rules with commands such as, "You must answer me at once when I speak to you." And ten years into the marriage, after becoming world famous for his theory of relativity in 1905, Einstein said of his wife, "I treat her as an employee whom I cannot fire." A year earlier, Mileva posed a penetrating question of her own to her friend Helene Savic, "All that fame does not leave a lot of time for a wife. But what can be done, one person gets the pearl and the other just gets the shell?"[5]

> You can't build a reputation on what you are going to do.
>
> **Henry Ford**

Needless to say, Einstein certainly had the capacity for empathy. He practiced it widely with others. But when it came to his own home, he didn't even try. So at age forty-four, Mileva was divorced and chronically ill. Hans Albert, their oldest son, was fifteen and bitter. Eduard, their second child, was nine and confused. And Albert was forty, a world-famous figure and married for a second time. The Einsteins' home could have been very different, had Albert only tried.

Don't make the same mistake. Remember what Clement Stone once said, "Try, try, try, and keep on trying is the rule that must be followed to become an expert in anything." Don't be discouraged if you're not an instant expert in empathy after reading this book. Keep trying. Every effort brings you closer to the marriage you desire.

Some Never Trade Places Because They Don't Make It a Priority

Some time ago, we attended a conference in Atlanta and heard Tim Sanders, former chief solutions officer at Yahoo! and author of *Love Is the Killer App*, speak. In his remarks he shared a piece on priorities that got us thinking.

"Take your life and all the things that you think are important, and put them in one of three categories," Tim suggested. Then he gave us the categories. They were represented by three items: glass, metal, and rubber.

The things that are made of rubber, when you drop them, he said, will bounce back. Nothing really happens when these kinds of things get dropped. So, for instance, if you miss your favorite team's game, your life will bounce back just fine. It doesn't change anything of consequence and nothing is lost. Missing a game or even a whole season of football will not alter your marriage or your spiritual life.

Things that are made of metal, when they get dropped, create a lot of noise. But you can recover from the drop. You miss a meeting at work, you can get the notes from a colleague. Or if you forget to balance your checkbook and lose track of how much you have in your account, and the bank notifies you that you have been spending more than you have — that's going to create a little bit of noise in your marriage, but you can recover from it.

Then there are things made of glass. And when you drop one of these, it will shatter into pieces and never be the same. Even though you can piece it back together, it will still be missing some pieces. It certainly won't look the same, and you probably won't be able to fill it up with water, because the consequences of it be being broken will forever affect how it's used.

> Action expresses priorities.
>
> **Charles A. Garfield**

Once Tim shared these vivid images with the audience, the room was hushed. He leaned over the podium and said this: "You're the only person who knows what those things are that you can't afford to drop. More than likely, they have a lot to do with your relationships. Your marriage, your family, and your friends."

We doubt you'd argue with that. The very fact that you're reading this book tells us your marriage is a priority. But what we don't know for sure is whether you're willing to establish mutual empathy as a priority. To be honest, we've met with plenty of couples who say they prize their marriage but who don't prioritize trading places. And as we've pointed out early on in this book, empathy requires intention.

Oil tycoon H. L. Hunt put it this way: "You've got to decide what you want, de-cide what you are willing to exchange for it. Establish your priorities and go to work." Some couples miss out on the ben-efits of trading places because they never establish it as a priority and they never go to work on it. Don't let that be said of you. Mu-tual empathy, in our opinion, is a priority that should be put into the glass category, to be treated with great care, because it gets to the heart of your marriage.

> Ever tried. Ever failed.
> No matter. Try Again.
> Fail again. Fail better.
>
> **Samuel Beckett**

Some Couples Never Trade Places Because They Aren't Willing to Change

In mid-December 1970, psychologists John Darley and C. Dan-iel Batson conducted an experiment at Princeton that has been replicated in hundreds of social psychology classes at universities since then. The study was inspired by the parable of the good Sa-maritan. In the biblical story, thieves beat and rob a man traveling from Jerusalem to Jericho, leaving him naked and half dead by the side of the road. A priest passes by and crosses the road rather than help the wounded traveler, and a Levite, a religious leader, does the same. Then a Samaritan — in those days a religious out-cast — comes upon the scene, applies balm and bandages to the victim's wounds, loads him on a donkey, brings him to an inn, nurses him through the night, and the following morning leaves money with the innkeeper for the traveler's continued care.

Darley and Batson decided to create a contemporary scenario with seminary students. A group of students at Princeton Theological Seminary was told that they were to go across campus to deliver a sermon on the topic of the good Samaritan. As part of the research, some of these students were told that they were late and needed to hurry up. Along their route across campus, Darley and Batson had hired an actor to play the role of a victim who was coughing and suffering, a person in obvious need of help.

Ninety percent of the "late" seminary students ignored the needs of the suffering person in their haste to get across campus. As the study reports, "Indeed, on several occasions, a seminary student going to give his talk on the parable of the good Samaritan literally stepped over the victim as he hurried away!"[6]

Think of that! These students were about to deliver a message on helping hurting people and they didn't practice their own message just minutes before they were to preach it.

The sad truth is that the same can happen with couples who intend to practice mutual empathy. You can understand how to empathize (even read a book on it). You can be highly motivated to empathize. And you can even talk about making mutual empathy a priority in your marriage. But if you aren't willing to change, you'll never put empathy into practice.

> I am always doing things I can't do, that's how I get to do them.
>
> **Pablo Picasso**

Why? Because empathy requires change. You see, once you empathize with your spouse, you become a different person, maybe slightly, maybe significantly. But be assured, you change. You don't look at your spouse the same way again. Every act of accurate empathy is like a little carving from a sculptor's chisel, causing you to have a slightly new perspective. It can't be helped. When you imagine, with both your head and your heart, what life must be like in your spouse's skin, you change. Empathy shapes you. It fashions a heart that is more closely aligned with your spouse's.

Feeling Each Other's Hearts

We've come a long way together in this book. We've looked at the two sides of trading places, your head and your heart. We've shown you how understanding your own emotional terrain is the prerequisite for empathy. We've given you a three-step plan for putting empathy into practice. And we've given you some practical ways to trade places starting today. But we want to leave you with one final word, an encouraging word.

No matter what your empathic ability is right now, it's going to get better. Why? Because empathy improves with time. It's honed by each year of your marriage.

In August of 2006, *Newsweek* magazine profiled the lives of Ruth and Billy Graham—not their historic crusades and international impact, but their life as an elderly couple approaching their final chapters on earth. As we read the article together, we were struck by the incredible quality of their marriage. "At night we have time together," Billy says. "We pray together and read the Bible together every night. It's a wonderful period of life for both of us. We've never had a love like we do now—we feel each other's hearts."[7]

That's what happens with mutual empathy. You feel each other's hearts. Love deepens. It even leaves its mark on your faces. Did you know that couples who practice trading places come to resemble each other? It's the result of sculpting your muscles as they evoke the same emotions over the years.[8] As the two of you smile or frown in unison, for example, you strengthen the parallel sets of muscles, gradually molding similar

> I never felt I didn't have a chance to win.
>
> **Arnold Palmer**

ridges and wrinkles, making your faces appear more alike. Not only that, but studies reveal that these couples who have greater facial similarities are also happier in their marriages.

As we noted in an earlier chapter, it's known as the Michelangelo Phenomenon.[9] It turns out that mutual empathy helps us "sculpt" not only each other's faces, but the shape of our marriage as well. Of course, this assumes your willingness to move into your partner's heart. And if you do, we're convinced it will be the best move you'll ever make in your marriage.

APPENDIXES

How to Trade Places When Your Spouse Doesn't Want To

Let's be honest. Not every spouse is equally motivated to "work on their marriage." Not every spouse is motivated to read "another marriage book." And not every spouse is willing to even try something new like Trading Places.

So what can you do when your spouse shows no interest in being proactively empathic with you? You're likely to think, *What's the use?* In fact, we've counseled enough couples to know that if you have an unmotivated spouse, you may even be wondering whether or not you married the right person. Of course, you already know that's a dangerous question. As Gary Thomas says in his book, *Sacred Marriage*: "If we are serious about pursuing spiritual growth through marriage, we must convince ourselves to refrain from asking the spiritually dangerous question: 'Did I marry the right person?'"

So be careful if this question is seeping into your mind. And be encouraged. The benefits of your single-sided efforts are immense. Why? Because empathy is contagious. It won't be overnight, but almost assuredly over time, your spouse will notice a significant change in you as you practice trading places with him or her. And with that observation comes a curiosity. *What's going on here?* your spouse is apt to wonder. And that leads to a new perspective that eventually leads to new behaviors.

We often liken this process to a mobile that hangs from the ceiling. It may be at rest, balanced comfortably, until just one piece is moved even slightly. Then the whole thing swings and moves until it finds equilibrium. In other words, because one piece of the mobile is moved, the rest of it has to eventually move with it until it finds a new balance. The same is true in marriage. Sometimes it takes just one spouse to make a change. And that change eventually leads to a change in the whole marriage.

So as you read through the chapters of this book, you will find places where we speak of "mutual empathy"—and, of course, that's the goal. Empathy works wonders when it's on a two-way street. But if your partner is not there with you, don't lose heart. You may feel discouraged by his or her lack of motivation, but you'll almost certainly discover, in time, that your empathy has rubbed off. You will find that your empathy begets empathy from your spouse. All that's needed, in most cases, is patience—and a refocus from wondering whether you married the right person to a focus on *being* the right person.

A character in the Anne Tyler novel A *Patchwork Planet* comes to realize this too late. The book's thirty-two-year-old narrator has gone through a divorce and now works at an occupation that has him relating almost exclusively with elderly people. As he observes their long-standing marriages, he comes to a profound understanding:

> I was beginning to suspect that it made no difference whether they'd married the right person. Finally, you're just with who you're with. You've signed on with her, put in half a century with her, grown to know her as well as you know yourself or even better, and she's become the right person. Or the only person, might be more to the point.

I wish someone had told me that earlier. I'd have hung on then; I swear I would. I never would have driven Natalie to leave me.[1]

We'll say it again. Be encouraged. Hang in there. Your efforts to trade places with your spouse will pay off. In time you'll never wonder whether you married the right person. You'll find that by being the right person your spouse follows suit.

Trading Places
If You've Been Burned

*A Message for Personalizers
and Those Married to One*

In my medical psychology fellowship I (Les) often consulted with physicians who were treating patients suffering from terrible physical burns. Because the healing process is so excruciating and because the necessary treatment so painful, some burn patients simply cannot cope and give up trying. When the nurses transport them into large tanks where their burned skin is meticulously scrubbed to prevent dangerous infections, they holler, "Don't touch me! Just let me die!"

Some people—especially those who fall into the "Personalizer" category in chapter 1—suffer the same pain emotionally and resort to a similar sense of hopelessness in their relationships. Many have grown up, for example, in homes where a parent's mood was unpredictable and behavior physically abusive. Some suffered the abandonment that comes from the death of a family member. Many endured verbal abuse through such statements as, "You'll never amount to anything," "Can't you do anything right?" or "You are the most disgusting little creep who ever walked the face of the earth." Most experts agree, by the way, that verbal abuse can be just as destructive as physical abuse. As the saying goes, "The blow of a whip raises a welt, but a blow of the tongue crushes bones."

Some Personalizers have withstood early and harsh criticism that was more carefully camouflaged. Their parents, for example, may have wriggled out of cruel statements by saying, "I was only joking." Or their parents offered "helpful" advice that was actually meant as a put-down. As a Yiddish proverb says, "If you're out to beat a dog, you're sure to find a stick."

It is not that every Personalizer is a victim of abuse. When a Sympathizer burns out, when she has given until there is no more to give, for example, she will usually move into the Personalizer quadrant. The Analyzer who has had one too many of his plans turn sour may become a Personalizer and retreat to social isolation. Regardless of their background, Personalizers have become so disillusioned by the potential pain of relationships, they fade into the woodwork, preferring their own world to the risk of relationships.

Personalizers, in an attempt to avoid any possibility of emotional pain, withdraw from relationships and silently cry out: "Don't touch!"[1] They live out the words of the poignant song by Simon and Garfunkel in the sixties: "I am a rock, I am an island." The song is about building walls that nothing can penetrate, about having no need of friendship, because it causes pain, and about disdaining laughter and loving.

A Six-Step Plan for Personalizers

If you are a Personalizer, you undoubtedly know the pain of interpersonal friction. You are aware of the anxiety you often experience in relationships and the fears you carry about being used or mistreated by others.

The following steps are designed to help you move beyond your fear and guilt to enjoy the delights of healthy interpersonal connections.

1. Admit your deficit.

You are probably motivated more by fear and guilt than you are by love. Your desire for self-protection and your lack of self-worth keep you from receiving and giving the gift of love. This is the root of your relational struggles and little can be done to improve your situation until you face this deficit of love head on.

Love is a central condition of human existence. We need it for survival. We seek it for pleasure. We require it to lend meaning and purpose to our lives. Love is not an embellishment or a refinement on the human condition. It is not the icing on the cake; it *is* the cake.

You can overcome your deficit of love by trying to accurately understand the people around you — especially your spouse. As S. I. Hayakawa said, "It is only as we fully understand opinions and attitudes different from our own and the reasons for them that we better understand our own place in the scheme of things." You have the capacity to give and receive love; you simply need to learn how to tap into it. The remaining steps will help you do so.

2. Plug into a caring community.

A caring community is a powerful healing and growth agent. An African proverb says, "It takes a whole village to raise a child." It also takes a community to raise a Personalizer to a more positive level of relationships. Your struggles cannot be worked out in isolation. A group of caring people is needed to model and foster healthy relationships.

When a retarded child is born, Professor Stanley Hauerwas of Duke University has written, the religious question we should ask is not "Why does God permit mental retardation in his world?" but "What sort of a community should we become so that mental retardation need not be a barrier to a child's enjoying a gratifying life?"

Life's toughest struggles are eased in a caring community of loving people. While relationships admittedly cause us problems, they also bring us our greatest joy. Make an effort to involve yourself in a group of positive people. Join a club or attend a class in your church or neighborhood. A caring community will help you come to a place where you will recognize that other people may complicate your existence, but life without them is unbearably desolate.

3. Beware of your defenses.

Achilles, the Greek mythological hero, was noted for his strength and bravery. In *The Iliad*, his mother, Thetis, had a premonition that her son would die in battle. So she dipped him in the River Styx to make him invulnerable. Thetis held the infant by his heel while the rest of his body was immersed in the water. As fate would have it, a poison arrow shot by Apollo wounded Achilles in the heel, his only vulnerable spot, and caused his death.

The Personalizer seeks to be invulnerable. He wears psychological defenses like a suit of armor. It is all in vain, however. Everyone has a weak spot. Everyone has an Achilles' heel.

When your primary concern is maximum security, you will soon find yourself living in a prison. The anxiety and guilt you carry unconsciously drives you to protect yourself from others. Robert Frost gives helpful advice for Withholders: "Do not build a wall until you know what you are walling in and what you are walling out."

Whether you are aware of it or not, you are instinctively building walls between you and other people.[2] The bricks in your wall include the defenses of denial, projection, and repression. Beware of these psychological maneuvers and how you may be using them to avoid responsibility for your condition.

Love has no defenses and only after you begin to break down your psychological walls will you realize your full potential for enjoying love.

4. Find compassionate but honest feedback.

Henry Ward Beecher said, "No man can tell another his faults so as to benefit him, unless he loves him." If you are to climb over your defensive walls and learn to empathize with others, you will need a trusted guide, a mentor that will make the journey with you.

Ask yourself who has had the most positive influence in your life. Is it a schoolteacher? An aunt or uncle? A parent? A grandparent? A minister? An employer? A coach? Whoever it is, your reason for choosing this person probably has more to do with who they are and how they live than anything else. It is because you admire them.

While this step may be difficult to take, it can be your key to personal growth: Approach that person you respect and ask them about a mentoring relationship that would enable you to learn more about love. Of course being a mentee requires opening yourself to critical feedback. But a true mentor will only give you a compassionate critique to help you become better. A mentoring relationship establishes a sense of accountability for improvement and is a vital element for anyone serious about changing their ways.

Even Ebenezer Scrooge, in Charles Dickens' A *Christmas Carol*, had a "mentor" in Jacob Marley's ghost. Through their relationship, the miserly old man exclaimed, "I will not be the man I was," and he changed his relational ways.

5. Risk vulnerability.

There is no way around it: caring for others leaves us vulnerable to disappointment and rejection. Relationships are risky. Just as a child risks scraping a knee in climbing a tree, so do you and I risk emotional pain in entering into relationship.

There is no way we can live a rich life unless we are willing to repeatedly suffer grief, sadness, anger, agony, confusion, criticism, and rejection. As psychiatrist and author M. Scott Peck has said, "We cannot heal without being willing to be hurt."

Dr. Peck also said, "If Jesus taught us anything, he taught us that the way to salvation lies through vulnerability."[3] Take the risk of opening yourself to another person. Disclose your pain to someone (like your mentor or your spouse). The effect of vulnerability on others is almost always disarming. When we gird ourselves with psychological defenses and pretend to be something we are not, the people around us become defensive as well. When you are vulnerable, however, it sends a message of authenticity and invites people to disclose their fears and pains too. Vulnerability is the bridge into a genuine caring relationship and will lead you over the troubled waters of withholding.

6. Seek healing through professional help.

Every Personalizer can benefit from the objective help of a trained psychotherapist or counselor. One of the best ways to locate a competent counselor is to ask others in the helping profession if they know of a good referral. Physicians, ministers, nurses, and teachers often provide excellent referrals. Other informational sources include hospitals, community service societies, referral services, and local professional societies.

If you have grown up with painful memories that have never been resolved, we urge you to seek professional help. This final step may be the most important thing you do for yourself and the people in your life.

Mini Thesaurus of Feeling Words

All too often, in attempting to understand our own feelings, we lack the words to describe them. We describe ourselves as "happy," for instance, when our emotion of the moment might more exactly be characterized as "euphoric," or perhaps "amused." We might describe our emotion as "sad," when in fact, we are feeling "weary" or "inadequate."

When we fail to choose a word that captures our own feelings precisely, we lack self-awareness and this diminishes our capacity to trade places. For this reason we are providing in this appendix a list of feeling words. You can consider it a mini thesaurus of emotions. And we have them categorized as "Positive Feeling Words" and "Negative Feeling Words." Both groupings are presented in alphabetical order. Of course, this is not exhaustive, but the listing should provide a good starting place for increasing your personal repertoire of feeling words to help you capture your own emotions—and eventually those of your spouse.

Positive Feeling Words

☐ Accepted	☐ Cheerful	☐ Expectant
☐ Adequate	☐ Comfortable	☐ Expressive
☐ Admired	☐ Competent	☐ Fascinated
☐ Adored	☐ Composed	☐ Flabbergasted
☐ Adventurous	☐ Concerned	☐ Fortunate
☐ Affectionate	☐ Confident	☐ Free
☐ Affirmed	☐ Considerate	☐ Friendly
☐ Alert	☐ Consoled	☐ Fulfilled
☐ Alive	☐ Contented	☐ Generous
☐ Amazed	☐ Cordial	☐ Gentle
☐ Amused	☐ Courageous	☐ Giddy
☐ Animated	☐ Creative	☐ Glad
☐ Anxious	☐ Curious	☐ Graceful
☐ Appealing	☐ Daring	☐ Grateful
☐ Appeased	☐ Delighted	☐ Gregarious
☐ Appreciated	☐ Delirious	☐ Healthy
☐ Approved	☐ Deserving	☐ Hopeful
☐ Ardent	☐ Determined	☐ Hospitable
☐ Astonished	☐ Eager	☐ Important
☐ Attentive	☐ Ecstatic	☐ Impressed
☐ Attractive	☐ Effervescent	☐ Included
☐ Aware	☐ Elated	☐ Independent
☐ Awed	☐ Empathic	☐ Infatuated
☐ Beautiful	☐ Enamored	☐ Innocent
☐ Benevolent	☐ Enchanted	☐ Inquisitive
☐ Bewitched	☐ Encouraged	☐ Inspired
☐ Brave	☐ Energetic	☐ Intelligent
☐ Brilliant	☐ Enlightened	☐ Interested
☐ Bubbly	☐ Enriched	☐ Invigorated
☐ Calm	☐ Enthusiastic	☐ Joyful
☐ Capable	☐ Entranced	☐ Jubilant
☐ Captivated	☐ Esteemed	☐ Kind
☐ Caring	☐ Euphoric	☐ Liked
☐ Certain	☐ Excited	☐ Lively

☐ Loved	☐ Refreshed	☐ Sustained
☐ Lucky	☐ Relaxed	☐ Sympathetic
☐ Masterful	☐ Relieved	☐ Tenacious
☐ Needed	☐ Renewed	☐ Tender
☐ Open	☐ Respected	☐ Thankful
☐ Optimistic	☐ Responsive	☐ Thoughtful
☐ Outgoing	☐ Romantic	☐ Thrilled
☐ Passionate	☐ Safe	☐ Tranquil
☐ Patient	☐ Satisfied	☐ Triumphant
☐ Peaceful	☐ Secure	☐ Trusted
☐ Pensive	☐ Seductive	☐ Understood
☐ Perceptive	☐ Sensitive	☐ Unencumbered
☐ Pleased	☐ Sentimental	☐ Untroubled
☐ Poised	☐ Serene	☐ Uplifted
☐ Popular	☐ Sincere	☐ Valiant
☐ Positive	☐ Smart	☐ Vibrant
☐ Powerful	☐ Sociable	☐ Victorious
☐ Productive	☐ Spiritual	☐ Vivacious
☐ Prosperous	☐ Stimulated	☐ Wanted
☐ Protected	☐ Strong	☐ Warm
☐ Proud	☐ Successful	☐ Welcomed
☐ Purposeful	☐ Supported	☐ Well
☐ Quiet	☐ Sure	☐ Worthy
☐ Receptive	☐ Surprised	☐ Zealous

Negative Feeling Words

☐ Abandoned	☐ Cynical	☐ Fidgety
☐ Afraid	☐ Dead	☐ Forlorn
☐ Agitated	☐ Defeated	☐ Frantic
☐ Alarmed	☐ Degraded	☐ Frightened
☐ Alienated	☐ Dejected	☐ Frozen
☐ Alone	☐ Dependent	☐ Frustrated
☐ Angry	☐ Depressed	☐ Fuming
☐ Annoyed	☐ Desperate	☐ Furious
☐ Antagonistic	☐ Despised	☐ Gloomy
☐ Anxious	☐ Detested	☐ Guilty
☐ Apathetic	☐ Disappointed	☐ Hated
☐ Appalled	☐ Discontented	☐ Headstrong
☐ Apprehensive	☐ Discouraged	☐ Helpless
☐ Arrogant	☐ Disdainful	☐ Hopeless
☐ Ashamed	☐ Disgusted	☐ Horrified
☐ Avoided	☐ Disinterested	☐ Hostile
☐ Bad	☐ Disliked	☐ Humiliated
☐ Bashful	☐ Dismayed	☐ Hurt
☐ Belittled	☐ Dissatisfied	☐ Hysterical
☐ Bewildered	☐ Distressed	☐ Ignored
☐ Bitter	☐ Disturbed	☐ Immobilized
☐ Bored	☐ Dreadful	☐ Impatient
☐ Bothered	☐ Dull	☐ Impetuous
☐ Burdensome	☐ Edgy	☐ Impotent
☐ Caged	☐ Embarrassed	☐ Impulsive
☐ Callous	☐ Emotional	☐ Inadequate
☐ Cautious	☐ Envious	☐ Incapable
☐ Censored	☐ Estranged	☐ Indifferent
☐ Cold	☐ Exhausted	☐ Indignant
☐ Confused	☐ Exploited	☐ Ineffectual
☐ Conquered	☐ Failed	☐ Inferior
☐ Contemptuous	☐ Fatigued	☐ Inhibited
☐ Controlled	☐ Fearful	☐ Injured
☐ Cornered	☐ Fed up	☐ Insecure

☐ Irritated
☐ Isolated
☐ Jealous
☐ Lethargic
☐ Listless
☐ Livid
☐ Lonely
☐ Mad
☐ Managed
☐ Maneuvered
☐ Manipulated
☐ Meddlesome
☐ Melancholy
☐ Miserable
☐ Moody
☐ Morose
☐ Mortified
☐ Naughty
☐ Negative
☐ Neglected
☐ Nervous
☐ Numb
☐ Obtuse
☐ Overpowered
☐ Pained
☐ Panicky
☐ Paralyzed
☐ Passive
☐ Perplexed
☐ Perturbed
☐ Pessimistic
☐ Pestered
☐ Pitying
☐ Placated
☐ Powerless

☐ Pressured
☐ Provoked
☐ Regretful
☐ Rejected
☐ Reluctant
☐ Repelled
☐ Repressed
☐ Repulsed
☐ Resentful
☐ Resigned
☐ Resistant
☐ Restless
☐ Restrained
☐ Sad
☐ Scared
☐ Seething
☐ Self-conscious
☐ Sensitive
☐ Shaken
☐ Shamed
☐ Shocked
☐ Shy
☐ Sick
☐ Stiff
☐ Stifled
☐ Stubborn
☐ Stunned
☐ Subdued
☐ Submissive
☐ Sullen
☐ Superior
☐ Suspicious
☐ Tense
☐ Terrified
☐ Threatened

☐ Thwarted
☐ Timid
☐ Tired
☐ Tolerated
☐ Tormented
☐ Tortured
☐ Touchy
☐ Trapped
☐ Troubled
☐ Unacceptable
☐ Unbalanced
☐ Uncaring
☐ Uncomfortable
☐ Unconcerned
☐ Uneasy
☐ Unfeeling
☐ Unimportant
☐ Unloved
☐ Unreasonable
☐ Unwanted
☐ Unwelcome
☐ Unworthy
☐ Upset
☐ Uptight
☐ Used
☐ Useless
☐ Vengeful
☐ Vulnerable
☐ Weak
☐ Weary
☐ Wild
☐ Withdrawn
☐ Worried
☐ Worthless

Visit www.realrelationships.com
for a FREE download of
the Trading Places card.

Three Steps to Trading Places

1. I Notice You
Set Aside Your Own Agenda

2. I Feel with You
Turn on Your Emotional Radar

3. I Act to Help You
Demonstrate Your Care Quotient

Notes

CHAPTER 1
The Two Sides of Trading Places

1. See Daniel Goleman's groundbreaking book, *Social Intelligence* (New York: Bantam, 2007) where he unpacks in detail the new science of human relationships.

2. See Stuart Ablon and Carl Marci, "Psychotherapy Process: The Missing Link," *Psychological Bulletin* 130 (2004): 664–68; Carl Marci, "Physiologic Evidence for the Interpersonal Role of Laughter During Psychotherapy," *Journal of Nervous and Mental Disease* 192 (2004): 689–95.

3. J. S. Morris, "Differential Extrageniculostriate and Amygdala Responses to Presentation and Emotional Faces in a Cortically Blind Field," *Brain* 124, no. 6 (2001): 1241–52.

CHAPTER 2
What Trading Places Will Do for Your Marriage

1. E. Newton, "Overconfidence in the Communication of Intent: Heard and Unheard Melodies" (PhD diss., Stanford University, 1990).

2. www.msnbc.com.

3. Amy Sutherland, "What Shamu Taught Me About a Happy Marriage," *New York Times*, June 25, 2006.

4. Rachel A. Simmons, Peter C. Gordon, and Dianne L. Chambless, "Pronouns in Marital Interaction: What Do 'You'and 'I' Say about Marital Health?" *Psychological Science* 16, no. 12 (December 2005): 932–36.

5. Tom Rath, *Vital Friends: The People You Can't Afford to Live Without* (New York: Gallup Press, 2006), 29.

6. Barbara Brown Taylor, *The Best Spiritual Writing*, ed. Phillip Zaleski (San Francisco: Harper, 1999), 262.

7. "A Linebacker's Tough Choice," *Christianity Today*, January/February 2001, www.christianitytoday.com.

8. Victor Bissonette, "Empathic Accuracy and Marital Conflict Resolution," in *Empathic Accuracy*, ed. William Ickes (New York: Guilford Press, 1997).

9. Janice Kiecolt-Glaser, "Marital Stress: Immunologic, Neuroendocrine, and Autonomic Correlates," *Annals of the New York Academy of Sciences* 840 (1999): 656–63.

10. Ibid., 657.

11. Robert Roy Britt, "Marital Spats Slow Healing of Wounds," *LiveScience*, December 5, 2005, www.livescience.com.

12. J. A. Coan, "Spouse, but Not Stranger, Hand Holding Attenuates Activation in Neural Systems Underlying Response to Threat," *Psychophysiology* 42 (2005): 44.

13. David Jeremiah, *Acts of Love: The Power of Encouragement* (Gresham, Ore.: Vision House, 1994).

14. Frank Bernieri and Robert Rosenthal, "Interpersonal Coordination, Behavior Matching, and Interpersonal Synchrony," in *Fundamentals of Nonverbal Behavior*, eds. Robert Feldman and Bernard Rime (Cambridge: Cambridge Univ. Press, 1991).

15. John C. Maxwell, *Winning with People* (Nashville: Nelson, 2004), 73.

16. H. B. Beckman and R. M. Frankel, "The Effect of Physician Behavior on the Collection of Data," *Annals of Internal Medicine* 101 (1984).

17. Wendy Levinson, "Physician-Patient Communication: The Relationship with Malpractice Claims Among Primary Care Physicians and Surgeons," *Journal of the American Medical Association* (February 19, 1997).

CHAPTER 3

The Prerequisite for Trading Places

1. Robert Levenson and Anna Ruef, "Empathy: A Physiological Substrate," *Journal of Personality and Social Psychology* 63, no. 2 (1992).

2. R. D. Lane and G. E. Schwartz, "Levels of emotional awareness: A cognitive-developmental theory and its application to psychopathology," *American Journal of Psychiatry* 144 (1987): 133–43. This study purports that emotional awareness is the ability to recognize emotions in oneself and in others, and that it can range from simple awareness of physiological sensations to more differentiated and labeled experiences. For example, at a low level of emotional awareness, individuals may be unable to describe how they are feeling, or may simply be able to say they feel "good" or "bad." Being able to identify single, simple emotions such as "happy" or "angry" represents an increasing level of awareness. Being able to recognize and identify more specific and differentiated emotions, such as guilt, disappointment, or resentment represents yet another increase in level of awareness. Finally, being able to identify differentiated emotions and to recognize that more than one emotion is present at a given time represents an even higher level of awareness. The following statement is an example of this level of awareness: "I feel disappointed

that we won't be able to see each other today, but glad that you're getting to leave early on vacation."

3. C. E. Mitchell, "Teaching to speak in feelings as a second language," *Family Therapy* 15 (1988): 75–81.

4. Kristin L. Croyle and Jennifer Waltz, "Emotional awareness and couples' relationship satisfaction," *Journal of Marital and Family Therapy* (October 2002).

5. Joseph LeDoux, *The Emotional Brain* (New York: Simon and Schuster, 1996).

6. R. D. Lane, E. M. Reiman, B. Axelrod, L. S. Yun, A. Holmes, and G. E. Schwartz, "Neural correlates of levels of emotional awareness: Evidence of an interaction between emotion and attention in the anterior cingulate cortex," *Journal of Cognitive Neuroscience* 10 (1998): 525–35.

7. J. M. Gottman and R. W. Levenson, "The Social Psychophysiology of Marriage," in *Perspectives on Marital Interaction*, eds. P. Noller and M. A. Fitzpatrick (Cleveland, UK: Multilingual Matters, 1988), 182–200.

8. Emily Butler, "The Social Consequences of Expressive Suppression," *Emotion* 3, no. 1 (2003): 48–67.

9. N. S. Jacobson, A. Christensen, S. E. Prince, J. Cordova, and K. Eldridge, "Integrative behavioral couple therapy: An acceptance-based, promising new treatment for couple discord," *Journal of Consulting and Clinical Psychology* 68 (2000): 351–55.

10. Oprah Winfrey, "What I Know for Sure," *O: The Oprah Magazine*, February 2002.

PART TWO
Three Crucial Steps to Trading Places

1. T. Connellan, *Inside the Magic Kingdom* (Atlanta: Bard Press, 1997).

2. Daniel Goleman, *Social Intelligence* (New York: Bantam, 2007), 58.

CHAPTER 4
I Notice You:
Setting Aside Your Own Agenda (Temporarily)

1. M. Voboril, "A Weighty Issue: Empathy suit shows medical personnel what it's like to be obese," *Newsday*, April 16, 2000.

2. See Birthways Childbirth Resource Center, Inc., www.empathybelly.org.

3. An analogous example comes from a study by Keysar and Henly (2002) in which participants read aloud several ambiguous sentences (such as "Angela killed the man with the gun") to another study participant. Speakers read the statement after reading a scenario that resolved the ambiguity of the sentence (e.g., indicated

whether the gun was the murder weapon or a possession of the victim), a scenario that was unavailable to listeners. As in the case of the tapping study, speakers assumed that what was obvious to them (i.e., the meaning of the sentence) would be obvious to the listener. Consistent with the speculation of Newton (1990) and Ross and Ward (1996), Keysar and Henly found that the overestimation was due, at least in part, to participants underestimating the ambiguity of their own utterances.

4. Other forms include:

egocentric myopia (the natural tendency to think absolutistically within an overly narrow point of view);

egocentric hypocrisy (the natural tendency to ignore flagrant inconsistencies between what we profess to believe and the actual beliefs our behavior imply, or inconsistencies between the standards to which we hold ourselves and those to which we expect others to adhere);

egocentric oversimplification (the natural tendency to ignore real and important complexities in the world in favor of simplistic notions when consideration of those complexities would require us to modify our beliefs or values);

egocentric blindness (the natural tendency not to notice facts or evidence which contradict our favored beliefs or values);

egocentric immediacy (the natural tendency to overgeneralize immediate feelings and experiences—so that when one event in our life is highly favorable or unfavorable, all of life seems favorable or unfavorable as well); and

egocentric absurdity (the natural tendency to fail to notice thinking which has "absurd" consequences, when noticing them would force us to rethink our position).

5. Sometimes you may not be fully aware of your own agenda without a serious look inward. That's where our unconscious agendas reside. These are the deep drives we have generated from unmet needs that started as early as childhood. Or they may be unconscious yearnings that were never met in a previous marriage. They could be unconscious desires from our dark side—things we don't even want to admit to ourselves, such as a hunger for attention or power. Of course, to bring these "agendas" to light, you often need the help of a counselor or mentor.

6. Edward Hallowell, "The Human Moment at Work," *Harvard Business Review* (January/February 1999), 59.

7. Paul R. Mendes-Flohr, ed. *A Land of Two Peoples: Martin Buber on Jews and Arabs* (New York: Oxford Univ. Press, 1983).

8. Martin Buber, *I and Thou*, trans. Walter Kaufmann, 1937 (New York: Simon & Schuster, 1990), 89.

9. Steve Moore, "A Graceful Goodbye," *Leadership* (Summer 2002), 41–42.

CHAPTER 5
I Feel with You:
Turning on Your Emotional Radar

1. C. J. Boyatzis and C. Satyaprasad, "Children's facial and gestural decoding and encoding: Relations between skills and with popularity," *Journal of Nonverbal Behavior* 18 (1994): 37–42.

2. P. Eckman and W. Friesen, *Unmasking the Face* (Englewood Cliffs, N.J.: Prentice Hall, 1975).

3. R. Rosenthal, J. Hall, M. R. DiMatteo, P. L. Rogers, and D. Archer, *Sensitivity to Nonverbal Communication: The PONS Test* (Baltimore: Johns Hopkins Univ. Press, 1979). See also, R. Rosenthal and R. L. Rosnow, *Essentials of Behavioral Research: Methods and Data Analysis* (New York: McGraw-Hill, 1991).

4. G. di Pelligrino, "Understanding Motor Events: A Neurophysiological Study," *Experimental Brain Research* 91 (1992): 176–80.

5. W. D. Hutchinson, "Pain-Related Neurons in the Human Cingulate Cortex," *Nature Neuroscience* 2 (1999): 403–5.

6. Giacomo Rizzolatti is quoted in Sandra Blakelee, "Cells that Read Minds," *New York Times*, January 10, 2006. See also, Giacomo Rizzolatti and M. A. Arbib, "Language within Our Grasp," *Trends in Neuroscience* 21 (1998): 188–94.

7. Albert Mehrabain, *Silent Messages: Implicit Communication of Emotions and Attitudes* (Belmont, Calif.: Wadsworth, 1981).

8. Laura Hillenbrand, "A Sudden Illness — How My Life Changed," *The New Yorker*, July 7, 2003.

9. R. C. Kessler, "The Costs of Caring: A Perspective on the Relationship Between Sex and Psychological Distress," in *Social Support: Theory, Research and Applications*, eds. I. G. Sarason and B. R. Sarason (Boston: Martinus Nijhoff, 1985), 491–507.

10. C. Heath and D. Heath, *Made to Stick* (New York: Random House, 2007), 127.

11. See J. Gottman, *The Relationship Cure* (New York: Crown, 2001), 170.

CHAPTER 6
I Act to Help You:
Demonstrating Your Care Quotient

1. Doug Kingsriter, "A Husband's Confession," *Christian Herald*, May/June 1991, 52.

2. Ap Dijksterhuis and John A. Bargh, "The Perception-behavior expressway: Automatic effects of social perception on social behavior," *Advances in Experimental Social Psychology* 33 (2001): 1–40.

3. Quoted in Dr. Paul Brand and Philip Yancey, *Fearfully & Wonderfully Made* (Grand Rapids: Zondervan, 1980).

4. *Time*, August 27, 1990, 38.

5. W. Litvack-Miller, D. McDougal, and D. M. Romney, "The structure of empathy during middle childhood and its relationship to prosocial behavior," *Genetic, Social, and Genetic Psychology Monographs* 123 (1997): 303–24.

6. Excerpt from *Fingerprints of God DVD Session 1*, by Jennifer Rothschild © Copyright 2005 LifeWay Press. All rights reserved. Used with permission.

7. Belden Lane, "Rabbinical Stories," *Christian Century* 98:41, December 16, 1981.

CHAPTER 7
Help Your Spouse See Your Side

1. David Mordkoff, "American Emmons Misses Out on Gold by Firing at Wrong Target," August 22, 2004, www.Sports.Yahoo.com.

2. C. Heath and D. Heath, *Made to Stick* (New York: Random House, 2007). See page 119 for how this exercise and principle apply to communicating any idea.

3. G. Thomas, "Feeling Let Down?" *Marriage Partnership*, Spring 2007, 46.

CONCLUSION
Why Every Couple Has a Chance at Trading Places

1. A Narcissist is classically defined as a person embodying traits and behaviors which signify obsession with one's self to the exclusion of others and the egotistic pursuit of one's own gratification, dominance, or ambition.

2. N. D. Feshback, "Studies of empathic behavior in children," in *The development of prosocial behavior*, ed. N. Eisenberg (New York: Academic Press, 1982), 315–38.

3. Beth Azar, "Defining the trait that makes us human," *APA Monitor* 28 (1997): 1.

4. Krista Tippett, *American Public Media: Speaking of Faith*, March 15, 2007, www.speakingoffaith.org/programs/einsteinethics/emailnewsletter20070315.shtml.

5. "Einstein's Wife." PBS Programming retrieved on April 20, 2007 from www.pbs.org/opb/einsteinswife/milevastory/married.htm.

6. Darley and Batson, "From Jerusalem to Jericho: A Study of Situational and Dispositional Variables in Helping Behavior," *Journal of Personality and Social Psychology* 27 (1973): 100–108.

7. Jon Meacham, "Pilgrim's Progress," *Newsweek*, August 14, 2006, 43.

8. R. B. Zajonc. "Convergence in the Physical Appearance of Spouses," *Motivation and Emotion* 11 (1987): 335–46.

9. S. M. Drigotasl, "Close Partner as Sculptor of the Ideal Self," *Journal of Personality and Social Psychology* 77 (1999): 293–323.

How to Trade Places When Your Spouse Doesn't Want To

1. Quoted in Gary Thomas, *Sacred Marriage* (Grand Rapids: Zondervan, 2000), 124.

Trading Places If You've Been Burned

1. C. U. Shantz, "Empathy in Relation to Social Cognitive Development," *The Counseling Psychologist* 5, no. 2 (1975).

2. James W. Pennebaker, PhD, *Opening Up: The Healing Power of Confiding in Others* (New York: Morrow, 1990).

3. M. Scott Peck, *The Road Less Traveled* (1978; repr. New York: Simon and Schuster, 2002).

About the Authors

Drs. Les and Leslie Parrott are founders and codirectors of the Center for Relationship Development at Seattle Pacific University (SPU), a groundbreaking program dedicated to teaching the basics of good relationships. Les Parrott is a professor of psychology at SPU, and Leslie is a marriage and family therapist at SPU. The Parrotts are authors of *Becoming Soul Mates*, *Your Time-Starved Marriage*, *Love Talk*, *The Parent You Want to Be*, and the Gold Medallion Award-winning *Saving Your Marriage Before It Starts*. The Parrotts have been featured on *Oprah*, *CBS This Morning*, CNN, and *The View*, and in *USA Today* and the *New York Times*. They are also frequent guest speakers and have written for a variety of magazines. The Parrotts' radio program, *Love Talk*, can be heard on stations throughout North America. Their website, RealRelationships. com, features more than one thousand free video-on-demand pieces answering relationship questions. Les and Leslie live in Seattle, Washington, with their two sons.

The Complete Guide to Marriage Mentoring

Connecting Couples to Build Better Marriages

Drs. Les and Leslie Parrott

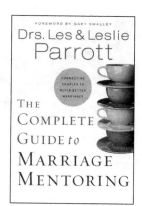

A comprehensive resource to help churches build a thriving marriage mentoring program.

Les and Leslie Parrott are passionate about how marriage mentoring can transform couples, families, and entire congregations. *The Complete Guide to Marriage Mentoring* includes life-changing insights and essential skills for

- Preparing engaged and newlywed couples
- Maximizing marriages from good to great
- Repairing marriages in distress

Practical guidelines help mentors and couples work together as a team, agree on outcomes, and develop skills for the marriage mentoring process. Appendixes offer a wealth of additional resources and tools. An exhaustive resource for marriage mentorship in any church setting, this guide also includes insights from interviews with church leaders and marriage mentors from around the country.

"The time is ripe for marriage mentoring, and this book is exactly what we need."

— Gary Smalley, author of *The DNA of Relationships*

Hardcover, Printed 978-0-310-27046-1

Also Available:

978-0-310-27047-8	51 Creative Ideas for Marriage Mentors	Softcover
978-0-310-27110-9	Complete Resource Kit for Marriage Mentoring, The	Curriculum Kit
978-0-310-27165-9	Marriage Mentor Training Manual for Husbands	Softcover
978-0-310-27125-3	Marriage Mentor Training Manual for Wives	Softcover

Pick up a copy today at your favorite bookstore!

ZONDERVAN®
.com

Love Talk

Speak Each Other's Language Like You Never Have Before

Drs. Les and Leslie Parrott

A breakthrough discovery in communication for transforming love relationships.

Over and over, couples consistently name "improved communication" as the greatest need in their relationships. *Love Talk*, by acclaimed relationship experts Drs. Les and Leslie Parrott, is a deep yet simple plan full of new insights that will revolutionize communication in love relationships.

In this no-nonsense book, "psychobabble" is translated into easy-to-understand language that clearly teaches you what you need to do — and not do — in order to speak each other's language like you never have before.

Love Talk includes:

- The Love Talk Indicator, a free personalized online assessment (a $30.00 value) to help you determine your unique talk style
- The Secret to Emotional Connection
- Charts and sample conversations
- The most important conversation you'll ever have
- A short course on Communication 101
- Appendix on Practical Help for the "Silent Partner"

Two softcover his and hers workbooks are full of lively exercises and enlightening self-tests that help couples apply what they are learning about communication directly to their relationships.

Hardcover, Jacketed 978-0-310-24596-4

Also Available:

978-0-310-26214-5	Love Talk	Audio CD, Abridged
978-0-310-26467-5	Love Talk Curriculum Kit	DVD
978-0-310-81047-6	Love Talk Starters	Mass Market
978-0-310-26212-1	Love Talk Workbook for Men	Softcover
978-0-310-26213-8	Love Talk Workbook for Women	Softcover

I Love You More

How Everyday Problems Can Strengthen Your Marriage

Drs. Les and Leslie Parrott

How to make the thorns in your marriage come up roses.

The big and little annoyances in your marriage are actually opportunities to deepen your love for each other. Relationship experts and award-winning authors Les and Leslie Parrott believe that your personal quirks and differences — where you squeeze the toothpaste tube, how you handle money — can actually help draw you together provided you handle them correctly.

Turn your marriage's prickly issues into opportunities to love each other more as you learn how to:

- build intimacy while respecting personal space
- tap the power of a positive marriage attitude
- replace boredom with fun, irritability with patience, busyness with time together, debt with a team approach to your finances ... and much, much more.

Plus — get an inside look at the very soul of your marriage, and how connecting with God can connect you to each other in ways you never dreamed.

Softcover: 978-0-310-25738-7

Also Available:

978-0-310-26582-5	I Love You More Curriculum Kit	DVD
978-0-310-26275-6	I Love You More Workbook for Men	Softcover
978-0-310-26276-3	I Love You More Workbook for Women	Softcover

Pick up a copy today at your favorite bookstore!

Your Time-Starved Marriage

How to Stay Connected at the Speed of Life

Drs. Les and Leslie Parrott

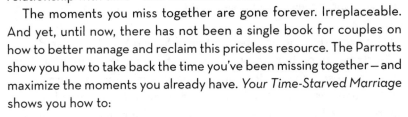

This is not a book about being more productive — it's a book about being more connected as a couple. In *Your Time-Starved Marriage,* Drs. Les and Leslie Parrott show how you can create a more fulfilling relationship with time — and with each other.

The moments you miss together are gone forever. Irreplaceable. And yet, until now, there has not been a single book for couples on how to better manage and reclaim this priceless resource. The Parrotts show you how to take back the time you've been missing together — and maximize the moments you already have. *Your Time-Starved Marriage* shows you how to:

- relate to time in a new way as a couple
- understand two lies every time-starved couple so easily believes
- slay the "busyness" giant that threatens your relationship
- integrate your time-style with a step-by-step approach that helps you make more time together
- stop the "time bandits" that steal your minutes
- maximize mealtime, money time, and leisure time
- reclaim all the free time you've been throwing away

Your Time-Starved Marriage gives you tools to feed your time-starved relationship, allowing you to maximize the moments you have together and enjoy them more.

Hardcover, Jacketed: 978-0-310-24597-1

Also Available:

978-0-310-81053-7	Time Together	Hardcover, Jacketed
978-0-310-26885-7	Your Time-Starved Marriage	Audio CD, Unabridged
978-0-310-27103-1	Your Time-Starved Marriage Groupware DVD	DVD
978-0-310-27155-0	Your Time-Starved Marriage Workbook for Men	Softcover
978-0-310-26729-4	Your Time-Starved Marriage Workbook for Women	Softcover

Saving Your Marriage Before It Starts

Seven Questions to Ask Before — and After — You Marry

Drs. Les and Leslie Parrott

A trusted marriage resource for engaged and newlywed couples is now expanded and updated.

With more than 500,000 copies in print, *Saving Your Marriage Before It Starts* has become the gold standard for helping today's engaged and newlywed couples build a solid foundation for lifelong love.

This expanded and updated edition of *Saving Your Marriage Before It Starts* has been honed by ten years of feedback, professional experience, research, and insight, making this tried-and-true resource better than ever. Specifically designed to meet the needs of today's couples, this book equips readers for a lifelong marriage before it even starts.

The men's and women's workbooks include self-tests and exercises sure to bring about personal insight and help you apply what you learn. The seven-session DVD features the Parrotts' lively presentation as well as real-life couples, making this a tool you can use "right out of the box." Two additional sessions for second marriages are also included. The unabridged audio CD is read by the authors.

The Curriculum Kit includes DVD with Leader's Guide, hardcover book, workbooks for men and women, and *Saving Your Second Marriage Before It Starts* workbooks for men and women. All components, except for DVD, are also sold separately.

Curriculum Kit: 978-0-310-27180-2

Also Available:

978-0-310-26210-7	Saving Your Marriage Before It Starts	Audio CD, Unabridged
978-0-310-26565-8	Saving Your Marriage Before It Starts Workbook for Men	Softcover
978-0-310-26564-1	Saving Your Marriage Before It Starts Workbook for Women	Softcover
978-0-310-27585-5	Saving Your Second Marriage Before It Starts Workbook for Women	Softcover
978-0-310-27584-8	Saving Your Second Marriage Before It Starts Workbook for Men	Softcover

The Parent You Want to Be

Who You Are Matters More Than What You Do

Drs. Les and Leslie Parrott

Being a parent is the most important calling you will ever have — with the emphasis on being. This parenting book is unlike any other: it's a step-by-step guide to selecting and modeling the very traits that you want your child to have. Because, as the authors explain, parenting is more about who you are than what you do.

Children long to be like their parents. That's the secret behind this method of choosing your top traits — your "intentional traits" — and projecting them consistently.

What is the single most important question you can ask yourself as a parent? Find out in this book. You'll also learn the three-step method to avoid becoming the parent you don't want to be … how to hear what your child isn't saying … the single best way to teach a child patience … and much more.

Written in short, designed-for-busy-parent chapters, with self-tests and discussion questions, this book helps you select your top traits and make them stick. Filled with encouragement, inspiring examples, and warm personal stories from their own experiences with their children, this book offers the Parrotts' revolutionary road map to parenting success.

Hardcover, Jacketed: 978-0-310-27245-8
Audio CD, Unabridged: 978-0-310-27977-8
Audio Download, Unabridged: 978-0-310-27978-5

Pick up a copy today at your favorite bookstore!

You Matter More Than You Think

What a Woman Needs to Know about the Difference She Makes

Dr. Leslie Parrott

Am I making a difference?
Does my life matter?

"How can I make a difference when some days I can't even find my keys?" asks award-winning author Leslie Parrott. "I've never been accused of being methodical, orderly, or linear. So when it came to considering my years on this planet, I did so without a sharpened pencil and a pad of paper. Instead, I walked along Discovery Beach, just a few minutes from our home in Seattle.

"Strange, though. All I seemed to ever bring home from my walks on the beach were little pieces of sea glass. Finding these random pieces eventually became a fixation. And, strangely, with each piece I collected, I felt a sense of calm. What could this mean? What was I to discover from this unintentional collection?"

In this poignant and vulnerable book, Leslie shows you how each hodgepodge piece of your life, no matter how haphazard, represents a part of what you do and who you are. While on the surface, none of these pieces may seem to make a terribly dramatic impact, Leslie will show you how they are your life and how when they are collected into a jar — a loving human heart— they become a treasure.

Hardcover, Jacketed: 978-0-310-24598-8
Softcover: 978-0-310-32497-3

Pick up a copy today at your favorite bookstore!

3 Seconds

The Power of Thinking Twice

Les Parrott, PhD

Just three seconds. The time it takes to make a decision. That's all that lies between settling for "Whatever" ... or insisting on "Whatever it takes."

3 *Seconds* shows how to unleash the inner resources that can move you to a whole new level of success. It comes down to six predictable impulses that most of us automatically accept without a second thought. You can replace them with new impulses that lead toward impact and significance. For instance, it takes 3 *Seconds* to ...

Disown Your Helplessness: The First Impulse: "There's nothing I can do about it." The Second Impulse: "I can't do everything, but I can do something."

Quit Stewing and Start Doing: The First Impulse: "Someday I'm going to do that." The Second Impulse: "I'm diving in ... starting today."

Fuel Your Passion: The First Impulse: "I'll do what happens to come my way." The Second Impulse: "I'll do what I'm designed to do."

Inhale ... exhale ... the difference of your lifetime can begin in the space of a single breath. The decision is yours. Start today.

Hardcover, Jacketed: 978-0-310-27249-6

Pick up a copy today at your favorite bookstore!

Share Your Thoughts

With the Author: Your comments will be forwarded to the author when you send them to *zauthor@zondervan.com*.

With Zondervan: Submit your review of this book by writing to *zreview@zondervan.com*.

Free Online Resources at
www.zondervan.com

Zondervan AuthorTracker: Be notified whenever your favorite authors publish new books, go on tour, or post an update about what's happening in their lives at www.zondervan.com/ authortracker.

Daily Bible Verses and Devotions: Enrich your life with daily Bible verses or devotions that help you start every morning focused on God. Visit www.zondervan.com/newsletters.

Free Email Publications: Sign up for newsletters on Christian living, academic resources, church ministry, fiction, children's resources, and more. Visit www.zondervan.com/newsletters.

Zondervan Bible Search: Find and compare Bible passages in a variety of translations at www.zondervanbiblesearch.com.

Other Benefits: Register yourself to receive online benefits like coupons and special offers, or to participate in research.

ZONDERVAN®

ZONDERVAN.com/
AUTHORTRACKER
follow your favorite authors